W9-BHO-424

THE ART OF BIBLE TRANSLATION

THE ART OF

Bible Translation

Robert Alter

PRINCETON UNIVERSITY PRESS

PRINCETON & OXFORD

Requests for permission to reproduce material from this work
should be sent to permissions@press.princeton.edu

Published by Princeton University Press
41 William Street, Princeton, New Jersey 08540
6 Oxford Street, Woodstock, Oxfordshire OX20 1TR

press.princeton.edu

LCCN 2018963488
ISBN 978-0-691-18149-3

British Library Cataloging-in-Publication Data is available

Editorial: Fred Appel and Thalia Leaf
Production Editorial: Kathleen Cioffi
Jacket Design: Faceout Studio, Lindy Martin
Jacket Art and Texture: Shutterstock
Production: Erin Suydam
Publicity: Tayler Lord
Copyeditor: David Hornik

This book has been composed in Miller

Printed on acid-free paper. ∞

Printed in the United States of America

10 9 8 7 6 5 4 3 2 1

For Nitza and Ilana,

dear friends and always intelligent cheerleaders

CONTENTS

Autobiographical Prelude · ix

CHAPTER 1   The Eclipse of Bible Translation   1

CHAPTER 2   Syntax   27

CHAPTER 3   Word Choice   45

CHAPTER 4   Sound Play and Word Play   65

CHAPTER 5   Rhythm   82

CHAPTER 6   The Language of Dialogue   103

Suggested Readings · 123
Index · 125

AUTOBIOGRAPHICAL PRELUDE

MANY READERS OF THIS BOOK will be aware that I was engaged in translating the Bible for more than two decades, during which, I should add, I also continued to pursue my interests as a critic of modern fiction. Inevitably, what I have to say now about translating the Bible will in some sense be a defense of my own work, though it is more accurate to say that it is an argument for the necessity of what I have aspired to do, however uneven the achievement. Any translation of a great piece of writing is bound to be imperfect, and in what follows I will be offering some examples of imperfections in my own efforts. The practice of translation, as I have learned from experience, entails an endless series of compromises, some of them happy, some painful and not quite right because the translator has been unable to find an adequate English equivalent for what is happening—often brilliantly—in the original language. The reflections in this book, then, on translating the Bible are offered in a spirit of humility, not triumphalism, with the underlying point that I have tried to do in my English version of the Bible what other translators by and large have not seen the need to do because they have had at best only a patchy sense of the literary aspects of the Hebrew.

I came to the translation of the Bible through two different accidental circumstances. My training and the initial focus of my work as a scholar were on European and American literature from the eighteenth century to the present and on modern Hebrew literature. I had long been fascinated by biblical narrative (by the time I was twenty I had a good competence in ancient as well as modern Hebrew) but was unable to explain why it was so great when, in the strict economy it exercised, it seemed so spare and perhaps even simple. Some fifteen years into my career, having published three books on the novel, I began to think that I might be able to offer some partial account of the literary greatness of biblical narrative, and I wrote an article, which at the time I conceived entirely as a onetime foray into the subject, on the need for a rigorous literary perspective on the Bible, bolstering my rather feisty contentions with a close reading of Genesis 38–39. The extent of the response, most of it enthusiastic, took me by surprise. Well, I thought, I have a few more ideas on biblical narrative, so I might write another article. Before long four articles were in print, some of them putting forth ideas I hadn't realized I had to begin with. I was then in full momentum to produce a book on the subject, which became *The Art of Biblical Narrative* (1981). All along I imagined that I would get this biblical business out of my system and go back to writing on Stendhal, Flaubert, Dickens, Agnon, and Nabokov. The book, however, was widely reviewed and enthusiastically received, which encouraged me to begin work on a companion volume on biblical poetry. By that point I had slid down the slippery slope into biblical studies, where I continued to labor alongside my work on the novel.

The second accident occurred in 1993, when the amiable and astute Steve Forman, who was to become my editor at W. W. Norton, paid me a visit and asked whether I might be interested in doing a Norton Critical Edition, either of something from Kafka (on whom I had then recently written) or from the Bible. I should explain for those outside the academic world that the Norton Critical Editions are admirable teaching texts, providing helpful annotations to classical works and in the back-of-the-book section, a variety of ancillary materials—sources on which the writer drew, relevant correspondence, contemporaneous reviews, modern critical essays. I responded to Steve Forman's proposal enthusiastically but also imprudently. One could do a really good Norton Critical Edition of Genesis, I told him, because there was now an abundance of excellent critical and source materials for the back of the book, but the problem was that there was something wrong with all the existing translations, so that if I were to undertake such an edition, I would have to do my own English version.

After some discussion involving my always dependable agent, Georges Borchardt, and the people at Norton, we agreed on a book that would be a straight translation and not a Norton Critical Edition. Initially, I thought I would merely provide occasional translator's notes to explain word play that could not be conveyed in English or to alert readers to points in the text where the meaning of the Hebrew was uncertain. But I had not gotten halfway through the first chapter of Genesis before I discovered that there were all sorts of things going on in the Hebrew, many having to do with its literary shaping, that had not been discussed in the conventional commentaries and that I wanted to take up. I thus found myself launched on still another unintended enterprise, a commentary to accompany my translation. I have to say that this gave me a certain sense of connection with the great medieval Hebrew commentators—especially my two favorites, Rashi and Abraham ibn Ezra—whom I had admired since late adolescence. I found it rather amusing, a few years later, when John Updike, in a *New Yorker* review of my *Five Books of Moses*, wondered, rather querulously, why anybody needed the commentary, which made the book ponderously heavy to hold, since the King James Bible, after all, had done quite nicely without a commentary. Updike's objection, I would say, was an eminently Protestant way of thinking about the Bible, and also did not register an awareness that King James opposed the inclusion of a commentary because he feared it would provide a vehicle for anti-monarchic views, as had the marginal comments in the Geneva Bible before it.

When I began work on Genesis, I thought of it as a perhaps quixotic experiment. I was aspiring to get into English as much as possible of the literary mastery of the Hebrew, but, aware as I was of the vast differences in structure and semantic range between the two languages, I was afraid that what I was trying to do was unfeasible, and that everyone, including me, would hate the finished product. The completed translation, inevitably, was no more than an approximation of what I had in mind, but it turned out to be a better approximation than I had thought I could manage. The reviews were quite laudatory; even the sales were strong; and so I was encouraged to undertake more Bible translation.

Let me hasten to say that at the time I had no notion whatever of translating the entire Hebrew Bible. After Genesis, I decided to do my other favorite piece of biblical narrative, the David story (1 and 2 Samuel and 1 Kings 1–2). After its publication, Steve Forman came on a trip to San Francisco and, over a congenial dinner, asked whether I was interested in doing more Bible translation. I told him, yes, I was enjoying both the work itself and the critical response to it. What do you have in mind, he asked, to do next? I told him I could make a neat little volume of several short biblical books that I liked. He frowned and explained, quite reasonably, that there wasn't much marketing context for miscellaneous books of the Bible. He then took me aback by saying that, ideally, he and his colleagues at Norton would love me to translate the whole Hebrew Bible. Only four obvious words could answer such a proposal: give me a break. We continued our conversation, however, and ended up raising the possibility that I might do

The Five Books of Moses. Though a little daunted by Leviticus with its intricate regulations for animal sacrifice looming large at the center of *The Five Books*, I agreed, after a few weeks' reflection, to undertake this. When *The Five Books of Moses* appeared, perhaps because it is widely regarded as the foundation of the whole Bible, the translation was reviewed, at length and for the most part with acclaim, in almost all the major journals.

By this point I felt that the wind was at my back, and so I went on to translate Psalms, the Wisdom Books, the Former Prophets, and, finally, even that little volume of short biblical books that I had first proposed to Steve Forman. Through all this I had clung to my original notion that I was not going to undertake anything so foolhardy as to translate the entire Hebrew Bible, but by the time all these installments were in print, it dawned on me that I had in fact done almost two-thirds of it, and that one big final push, with the great challenge of the Prophets, a large, daunting bloc among the books as yet untranslated, could lead to encompassing the whole.

From the beginning my translation was impelled by a deep conviction that the literary style of the Bible in both the prose narratives and the poetry is not some sort of aesthetic embellishment of the "message" of Scripture but the vital medium through which the biblical vision of God, human nature, history, politics, society, and moral value is conveyed. In the chapters that follow, I will provide a variety of illustrations of this essential aspect of the Bible, but let me offer here one small example. The prophet Isaiah, who communicated his visions to the audiences of his time in what is often great poetry, was a master of word play. In order to express what he saw as the ghastly perversion of values in his society, he frequently juxtaposed in his poems two words that sounded almost alike but were opposite in meaning, with the intention of showing linguistically how his

Judahite contemporaries had turned moral values topsy-turvy, substituting evil for good, vice for virtue. Without the word play one misses the real point of these prophecies, and so I would contend that a translator must seek as much as it is feasible to create English equivalents. I will explore here how not only word play but also diction, rhythm, syntax, and the strategic choice of words are decisive elements in shaping the literary authority and conveying the moral and religious outlook of the Hebrew Bible. Considering all these challenges to the translator means that this book on translating the Bible also ends up being an overview of the principal aspects of biblical style, a topic to which, somewhat surprisingly, no existing book has been devoted.

My project was undertaken after the advent of e-mail, and that actually made a certain difference. With the convenience and swiftness of e-mail, readers are much more likely to write authors than in the era when we were all dependent on the postal services. During the years I was working on my translation I received hundreds of e-mails from readers—sometimes four or five in a single week. Some of these helpfully pointed out typos, to which I am dreadfully prone, or even places where my lazy eye had skipped over a word or phrase in the Hebrew. Some took issue with a particular translation choice— on occasion, justly, though usually I felt warranted in standing my ground and gave my reasons to the objector. The majority of these communications were to tell me how much my translation had meant to the person writing me, and that encouragement was a sustaining force in my long trek through the Bible.

I did not initially have a very clear sense of the audience to which my work was directed. My only thought was that I wanted to make the Bible available for English readers in language that might at least intimate something of the power, the subtlety, and the beauty of the Hebrew. The actual readership, as this electronic correspondence informed me, was broader and more varied than I would have imagined. I might have at first thought of readers who were chiefly literary, as indeed I am, and who through the translation would be able to enjoy more keenly the literary achievement of the Bible. But, as it turned out, I received enheartening words from Orthodox Jews, from a Methodist minister, from a Presbyterian organist, even from an Episcopalian nun who said that my translation of Psalms had changed her spiritual practice. Responses repeatedly came from unexpected quarters, such as the fourteen-year-old girl at a Jewish day school who told me in impressively literate English that she had come to trust my commentary more than any other. (I'm not sure I would agree with her, but what she said was certainly gratifying.) Through all this, then, I have developed a sense that my translation, whatever its imperfections, has begun to serve a cultural need for English readers interested in the Bible. That in turn has given me confidence to seek to explain in these chapters why central aspects of literary style in the Hebrew Bible have to be addressed in English translation, within the limits imposed by the disparities between the two languages, and to attempt to make clear what is lost in the failure to address the enlivening and determinative role of style in the Bible. In the chapters that follow I will try to explain how syntax, word choice, rhythm, sound play, word play, and diction are artfully deployed in the Hebrew and why, whatever challenges all these aspects of style pose, they need somehow to be reflected in translation. All this may throw some light on what should be involved in translating the Bible, and perhaps it will also convey some sense of the literary artistry of the biblical writers. Although the impetus for this book was definitely an attempt to consider the challenges of translating the Bible and how they might be met, the topics discussed ended up involving both proposals about literary translation and a general overview of the principal features of style in the Bible. As I have noted, no such study really exists, and that in itself is a symptom of the problem that these chapters seek to address.

THE ART OF BIBLE TRANSLATION

CHAPTER ONE

The Eclipse of Bible Translation

THE TRANSLATION OF THE BIBLE into English has had a peculiar history. The first complete translation of the New Testament as well as of extensive portions of the Old Testament from the original languages, and also the first after the invention of printing, was done by William Tyndale in the 1520s. His work, alas, was permanently interrupted when he was seized by the Inquisition, strangled (not quite successfully), and then burned at the stake. Catholic authorities in this period, it is clear, took a rather dim view of vernacular renderings of Scripture. Tyndale, who was clearly a translator of genius, favored a notion that there was an underlying affinity between the Hebrew and English languages, and as a result that it was possible to render the true meaning of the Bible in a way that would speak directly to an ordinary plowboy. One may regard this as a beguiling fiction that helped to make possible the remarkable achievement of his English version. The Tyndale Bible provided the basis a generation later for the Geneva Bible, produced by Protestant exiles who had fled to Switzerland during the reign of the militantly Catholic Queen Mary. More decisively, in the first decade of the seventeenth century Tyndale became the model for the King James Version (1611). The translators convened by King James took very many verses and countless phrases and clauses directly from Tyndale, but, even more important, he blazed a stylistic path for them even when they weren't copying him. An instructive case in point is their translation of Ecclesiastes. It is one of their most memorable achievements, capturing much of the haunting prose poetry of the Hebrew with its beautiful cadences (even if some of the key terms, such as "vanity of vanities" and "vexation of spirit," reflect a misunderstanding of the original). None of this is borrowed from Tyndale because he did not survive to translate Ecclesiastes, but in regard to diction and rhythm and the managing of many Hebrew idioms, he had given them an invaluable precedent.

It took a century or more before the King James Bible became the fully canonical English version. By the nineteenth century it was entirely dominant—some of the major works of American literature in this era are unthinkable without the matrix of the King James language—and, despite the welter of new translations that have been produced from then down to our own time, the 1611 translation has shown a surprising degree of staying power. As recently as 2014, it was still the preferred Bible of 55 percent of the respondents to a broad survey. It had undergone several successive revisions beginning in the later nineteenth century that mitigated the archaism of its language and corrected its more egregious translation errors while unfortunately somewhat flattening its style, but the grandeur of the original version, even if some of its language is now opaque, still clearly continues to appeal to a large number of readers. This preference for the King James Version is surely dictated in part by the woeful inadequacies of the twentieth-century English translations. Before considering the reasons for this general decline, I would like to indicate briefly the genuine virtues and also the shortcomings of what has for so long been our canonical English Bible.

The committees—they were called "companies"—assembled under the authority of King James were composed of scholars and ecclesiastical figures with impressive credentials of erudition—many knew Arabic and Syriac as well as Hebrew, Greek, and Aramaic—who were also immersed in the literary culture of their age. Launcelot Andrewes, the Anglican bishop who was probably the most influential figure among the company members, was one of the great prose stylists of the early seventeenth century, as his published sermons attest, and his fine command of the language surely left its imprint on the translation. The much-celebrated eloquence of the King James Version is very real, and that, coupled with its royal authorization, must have had a great deal to do with its rise to canonical status and with its profound influence on literary English.

One of the signal strengths of the 1611 translation is what I would call its inspired (not divinely inspired) literalism. The seventeenth-century translators worked with the theological conviction that every word of the Bible was revealed to humankind by God and that one didn't play games with God's words. A vivid typographical illustration of this conviction is the use of italics that has often puzzled modern readers. (In the 1611 printing it was less confusing because these words appeared in a roman font that contrasted with the more or less gothic font of the surrounding text.) The italics do not indicate emphasis, as they would in current practice, but rather the introduction into the translation of a word that is merely implied in the original. To cite a very common example, Hebrew has no present tense for the verb "to be." To say "I am Joseph," just two words are used—"I" (*'ani*) and "Joseph" (*Yosef*). The King James translators, given their scruples, could not permit themselves to write "am" as though it actually appeared in the Hebrew, and so they set out the word in a different typeface to show that it wasn't literally in the Hebrew but had to be added because of the necessities of English usage.

The inspired literalism of the King James Version begins with its representation of Hebrew syntax in the prose narratives. Biblical prose predominantly uses parataxis—that is, the ordering of words in parallel clauses linked by "and," with very little syntactic subordination or the accompanying subordinate conjunctions such as "because," "although," or "since" that specify the connection between clauses. (In some cases, however, there are clues of context or grammar that give this same Hebrew particle the sense of "but," and in those instances translators are obliged to render it as "but.") My guess is that the King James translators followed the Hebrew parataxis not chiefly out of a stylistic decision but because they thought that if this is the order in which God put the Hebrew words, that order should be reproduced in English. In the Hebrew, parataxis is very much an artful vehicle, generating imposing cadenced sequences of parallel clauses and often exploiting the lack of causal explanation of the relation between clauses to create thought-provoking ambiguities. This was not a normal way to organize language in English, but it would become a strong literary option after 1611. Most of this has been thrown out the window in the modern English versions, impelled by the misconception that modern readers cannot make sense of parataxis and that everything in the biblical text needs to be explained.

There is another aspect of style for which the King James translators came to a happy solution that has been almost universally jettisoned by their modern successors. Biblical narrative makes do with a very small vocabulary. My own inference is that there was a conventional understanding that only a certain limited vocabulary could be used for narrative prose. One

principal reason for this inference is that there are many terms
that appear in poetry but never in prose. In biblical narrative,
for example, there is only one word for light, *'or*, together with
a cognate, *ma'or*, that means "source of light" or "lamp." Biblical
poetry, on the other hand, exhibits a whole handful of more
elaborate or elevated words that would be the equivalents of
such English terms as "brilliance," "radiance," or "effulgence."
Telling a story rather than composing a poem in ancient Hebrew, you evidently were expected to refrain from such highfalutin language and restrict yourself to the primary term *'or*.
By and large, the King James translators respected this stylistic
practice whereas their modern successors have been impelled
either to translate repeated terms differently according to context or to improve on the original by substituting a fancy and
purportedly literary term or an explanatory one for the home-
spun Hebrew word.

Let me illustrate this lamentable trend in Bible translation
with two verses from Genesis (7:17–18). Here is the King James
Version: "And the flood was forty days upon the earth; and the
waters increased, and bare up the ark, and it was lift up above
the earth. And the waters prevailed, and were increased greatly
upon the earth; and the ark went upon the face of the waters."
All this should be perfectly intelligible to the modern reader,
with only the archaic form of two verbs a little strange. Now I
will cite, in order, Protestant, Catholic, and Jewish translations
done in the second half of the twentieth century. The Revised
English Bible: "The flood continued on the earth for forty days,
and the swelling waters lifted up the ark so that it was high
above the ground. The ark floated on the surface of the swollen
waters as they increased over the earth." The New Jerusalem
Bible: "The flood lasted forty days on earth. The waters swelled,
lifting the ark until it floated off the ground. The waters rose,
swelling above the ground, and the ark drifted away over the

waters." The Jewish Publication Society: "The Flood continued forty days on the earth and raised the ark so that it rose above the earth. The waters swelled and increased greatly upon the earth, and the ark drifted upon the waters."

It should be noted that all three modern versions do away with the parataxis of the Hebrew, introducing subordinate clauses ("so that . . .") and participial phrases where the original has independent clauses. In this fashion, the grand rhythm of parallel utterances is turned into something commonplace. I would especially like to direct attention here to the choices made for two verbs. The King James Version, faithfully following the Hebrew, has "the flood *was* forty days upon the earth" and "the ark *went* upon the face of the waters." To the modern translators this evidently seemed too simple, and so instead of "was" they use "continued" or "lasted," and instead of "went" they give us "floated" or "drifted." Such substitutions seriously compromise the beautiful dignity of the Hebrew with its adherence to a purposefully simple lexicon of primary terms. (The stylistic power of such simplicity was keenly understood by Hemingway, who of course was strongly influenced by the King James Version.) The actual picture of what is happening with the ark is also somewhat altered by these translators in their desire to "improve" it for the modern reader. One might perhaps infer that the ark was drifting, or drifting away, but the Hebrew does not actually say that, and this leads readers to the conclusion that Noah's ark was rudderless, which may or may not have been the case. In any event, the grand simplicity of "the ark went upon the face of the waters" is entirely lost. There is a sense that the modern biblical scholars who produced these versions drew on a literary experience limited to middlebrow magazine fiction, and so they labored under the illusion that they were making the Flood story more vivid for modern readers by introducing such locutions as "swollen waters" (a phrase that might appear in a conventional short story about the Mississippi flooding) and the ark drifting away. These translations are also informed by what I would characterize as a rage to explain the biblical text. Elsewhere, I might add, the impulse to explain through translation has still more dire consequences because it becomes an explanation to make the Bible conform to modern views or modern ideologies. In the present instance, the translators, apprehensive that readers might not understand what happens when the rain comes down and the waters go up, bearing the ark on their surface, spell out the mechanical steps of the process in explanatory subordinate clauses—"so that it was high above the ground," "until it floated off the ground," "so that it rose above the earth." This is manifestly not how the biblical writers chose to tell their stories.

This celebration of the achievement of the King James Version requires some serious qualification. There are two problems with the 1611 translation that are scarcely its fault. The English language, of course, has changed both lexically and grammatically in the course of four centuries. Apart from students of Renaissance literature, not many readers today will know, for example, that "froward" means "perverse" or "contrary," and that "ward" means "prison" or "custody." There is not much to be done about such difficulties except annotation, something Herbert Marks has provided in his splendid Norton Critical Edition of the King James Old Testament. The other pervasive problem with our canonical English version is that the seventeenth-century translators, for all their learning, had a rather imperfect grasp of biblical Hebrew. At times they get confused about the syntax, and they repeatedly miss the nuance, or even the actual meaning, of Hebrew words. Usually this is a matter of being slightly off or somewhat misleading, as when, following the Vulgate, they transpose concrete Hebrew terms into theologically fraught ones—"soul" for *nefesh*, which actually means "essential self," "being," "life-breath," or "salvation" for *yeshu'ah*, which means "rescue," "getting out of a tight fix." Sometimes, alas, there are real howlers. In the mysterious covenant between God and Abram in Genesis 15, the 1611 version reads "an horror of great darkness fell upon him," because they have taken an adjective, *hasheikhah* to be the noun it formally resembles. The Hebrew actually says "a great dark horror fell upon him," with no suggestion that Abram our forefather was afraid of the dark. Still more egregiously, in Job 3:8 we encounter cursers of the day "who are ready to raise up their mourning." The Hebrew in fact says "raise up Leviathan." The King James translators misread the mythological beast *lewayatan* as the rabbinic word for "funeral," *lewayah*, not distinguishing between biblical and rabbinic Hebrew, and overlooking the fact that the word as they incorrectly construed it would have an inappropriate feminine possessive suffix. Such errors are probably understandable because Hebrew was a book language for them, cultivated for barely a century by Christian humanists. By contrast, the great Hebrew commentators of the Middle Ages, such as Rashi and Abraham ibn Ezra, were immersed in Hebrew, thought in Hebrew, and—in the case of ibn Ezra—wrote poetry in Hebrew, and consequently had a much firmer command of syntax, grammar, and lexical nuance.

There is also a stylistic issue with the King James Version. It may be a little surprising to say that its treatment of poetry is by and large less successful than its representation of narrative prose. I would argue that this is often the case even when the lines of verse exhibit persuasive force, as they famously do in Psalms. Let me cite an instance that most English speakers know by heart, from the twenty-third psalm: "Yea, though I walk through the valley of the shadow of death, I will fear no evil." This is grand, but the grandeur is nothing like the Hebrew. Instead of eight words and thirteen syllables, *gam ki 'elekh begei' tsalmawet lo' 'ira r'a*, we are given seventeen words and twenty syllables. The power of biblical poetry inheres in its terrific compactness. The King James translators, attached to a more orotund and expansive Jacobean rhetoric, rarely produce English equivalents of this compactness. The English line from Psalms is a memorable line of poetry, but, stretching from margin to margin on the page, it reads more like a line from Walt Whitman (who of course was profoundly influenced by the King James Psalms) than like a line of ancient Hebrew verse. The underlying problem, I suspect, is that the King James translators, though they had an impressive feel for English, approached biblical Hebrew as a language to be deciphered from the printed page, and they often did not seem to *hear* it.

Here is a line of poetry from Job (3:11) that instructively illustrates both the remarkable stylistic strength and the weakness of the King James Version. The first half of the line—lines of biblical poetry usually show two inter-echoing halves, or "versets"—could scarcely be improved on: "Why died I not from the womb?" The Hebrew is *lamah lo' merehem 'amut*. As a translator, I envy the freedom of the King James collaborators to use a compact syntactic inversion, "died I not," whereas, working in the twenty-first century, I felt constrained to adopt the clumsier "did I not die." But in the second half of the line, alas, the translation unravels: "Why did I not give up the ghost when I came out of the belly?" These fifteen words—all but one monosyllabic but nonetheless arhythmic—represent three words, eight syllables, in the Hebrew: *mibeten yatsa'ti we'egwah*. The meaning of the Hebrew is there, but the poetry gets lost in the verbiage. My own approximation of the Hebrew is "from the belly come out, breathe my last." For the three final words, "expire" would have been rhythmically preferable, but it seemed to me too abstract and Latinate for the diction of the poem. As elsewhere, there is both gain and loss in translation choices.

The King James Bible, then, remains an imposing achievement, yet as I have indicated, it has its drawbacks. But why have English translators in our age fallen so steeply from this grand precedent? To begin with, I would note a pronounced tendency among them to throw out the beautiful baby with the bathwater. Those companies convened by King James, their modern successors assume, got it altogether wrong. We must now start from scratch, swerve away sharply from all that they did, treat biblical syntax in an informed way that can speak to modern readers, represent biblical terms with what we understand to be philological precision according to their shifting contexts, and make things entirely clear for people who want to know what the Bible is really saying. This impulse is misconceived on two grounds. First, the Bible itself does not generally exhibit the clarity to which its modern translators aspire: the Hebrew writers reveled in the proliferation of meanings, the cultivation of ambiguities, the playing of one sense of a term against another, and this richness is erased in the deceptive antiseptic clarity of the modern versions. The second issue is the historical momentum of the commanding precedent created by the King James Bible. It has been such a powerful presence for four centuries of English readers that a translation of the Bible that proceeds as though it simply didn't exist becomes hard to read as a version of the Bible that has any literary standing. I don't mean to advocate a direct imitation of the King James Bible, but I would propose that for an English translation to make literary sense it somehow has to register the stylistic authority of the 1611 version, or, one might say, it needs to create a modern transmutation of how the King James translators imagined the Bible should be rendered in English. When Stendhal was working on *The Charterhouse of Parma*, he noted that he would like it to read like Fielding's *Tom Jones*—not of course, he hastened to say, like the *Tom Jones* of the eighteenth century but as an equivalent to the style of that novel as it might be written in the 1830s, and that, I would propose, is what modern translators of the Bible should try to do in relation to the King James Version.

Equally important as a reason for the gravely flawed modern translations of the Bible is a problem of what might be characterized as the sociology of knowledge. Modern translators of Scripture are almost all rigorously trained at a few premier universities that have well-established programs in biblical studies. In the United States, these would include Harvard, Yale, Johns Hopkins, the University of Pennsylvania, and the University of Chicago. Doctoral students at these august institutions acquire the tools of philological analysis, study the complex evolution of the biblical texts, learn Akkadian, Ugaritic, and in some cases, Egyptian as well. All this is certainly helpful for reconstructing the elusive meanings of writings removed from us by nearly three millennia. The general commitment, however, to eliciting clarity from much that is obscure has the unfortunate consequence for translation of introducing clarifications that compromise the literary integrity of the biblical texts. One manifestation of this tendency, to which I have already alluded, is the practice of repeatedly assigning the same Hebrew term different English equivalents according to the contexts in which it appears, a practice that sometimes may be unavoidable but often is not. Another consequence of the impulse for clarification is to represent legal, medical, architectural, and other terms from specific realms of experience in purportedly precise modern technical language when the Hebrew by and large hews to general terms (the priest in Leviticus, for example, "sees" the symptoms of a skin disease while in the modern translations he "inspects" them).

Though the training of modern biblical scholars is quite strong in exploring all the ancient Near Eastern contexts relative to the Bible, attention to the literary aspects of the Bible, which are essential to understanding it, plays no role at all in this training. Granted, there have been efforts in recent decades by some biblical scholars to bring to bear literary perspectives in their work, but these remain marginal in the field. It is still inconceivable for a course to be offered in prose style or narrative conventions in any of the major institutions where there are programs in Hebrew Bible. Moreover, the scholars, largely trained in the middle decades of the previous century, who produced the various modern English versions would never have dreamed of addressing such questions. Literary style, then, is never studied, and the translators consequently proceed as if the Bible had no style at all, as if a translator were entitled to represent it in a hodgepodge of modern English styles. The conventions and techniques of biblical narrative, which are manifested in crucial word choices by the Hebrew writers, as I have noted, have no part in the curriculum of biblical studies, and, with just a few exceptions, the same is true of the forms of biblical poetry—a deficiency that is even visible typographically in the modern translations, which often lay out lines of verse arbitrarily in breaks that do not correspond to the actual Hebrew lines.

The blindness to the literary dimension of the ancient texts also compromises biblical philology as it is taught in these institutions and then reflected in the translations of their graduates. Recovering the meanings of biblical words is conceived as a matter of establishing lexical values, and very little thought is given to nuance, connotation, or level of diction. In the story, for example, of the rape of Tamar in 2 Samuel 13, the noun *biryah* and its cognate verb, repeatedly used in this episode and very rare elsewhere, is regularly represented by the modern translations, quite blandly, as "food." This is not, however, the normal biblical term for "food," and an inspection with the aid of a Hebrew concordance of all its occurrences reveals that it is invariably food offered to someone who has been fasting or who has been for some reason doing poorly, as Amnon in this story pretends to be doing. Thus an English equivalent such as "nourishment," which fits the narrative context and distinguishes this word from the usual term for "food," is required.

What this example should suggest is that you cannot determine the meanings of biblical words without taking into consideration their narrative or poetic contexts. The example from 2 Samuel 13 is an instance of missed nuance, but there are other cases in which the translators altogether misconstrue the meaning because of their insensitivity to the bearing of the narrative on the term. A striking case is the universal mistranslation of a rare Hebrew term, *halitsot*, in the Samson story (Judges 14:19). All the modern translators labor under the misapprehension that the reference is to a garment—the Jerusalem Bible: "what they wore"; the Jewish Publication Society (telescoping two different words in the Hebrew): "sets of clothing"; the Revised English Bible, quite fancifully, with no philological warrant, "their spoils." Now, this Hebrew word is followed immediately in the text by another that sounds a little like it, *halifot*, which unambiguously means "changes of garments." Samson's wager with the Philistine wedding guests had been that if they solved his riddle, he would give all thirty of them *halifot begadim*, "changes of garments." The translators all assume that *halitsot* also must mean some sort of garment. Instructively, *halitsot* as something worn, but not really a garment, appears just one other time in the Bible. In 2 Samuel 2:21, when Saul's general Abner is being pursued on the battlefield by the swift-footed Asahel, Abner tells him, "Swerve you to your right or to your left and seize for yourself one of the lads, and take you his *ḥalitsah*" (2 Samuel 2:21). The Revised English Bible people think this is a "belt"; the Jewish Publication Society proposes "tunic"; the Jerusalem Bible again fudges with "spoil." But any reader of the Iliad knows that what a warrior takes from his slain foe on the battlefield is not an item of apparel but his *armor*. (The King James translators actually got this right, perhaps because, unlike their successors, they were good readers of Homer, as were the Septuagint translators whom they followed, although they miss the meaning in the Samson story.) The root of the noun in question supports this conclusion. The word for military vanguard, *ḥaluts*, shows the same tri-consonantal root. What the warriors in the vanguard were wearing was *ḥalitsot*, armor. All this, moreover, throws piquant new light on a detail of the Samson story. His wager with the wedding guests was for *ḥalifot*, changes of garments. Infuriated by the trick they have played on him, he goes down to Gaza and kills not ordinary men in perhaps fancy robes but thirty warriors, and as a provocative gesture, he brings their armor, far more valuable than changes of garments, as payment to the thirty wedding guests. Attention, then, to what is going on in the narrative in both Judges 14 and 2 Samuel 2 yields an understanding of the meaning of the word, which in turn sharpens our perception of what is actually happening in the story. It is generally the case that there are livelier and more surprising details in the biblical stories than we first realize, but these get erased by translators who have an inadequate grasp of how the narratives work.

A consideration of literary context, not an activity promoted in biblical philology as it is generally practiced, can actually illuminate a crux in the biblical text. For readers unfamiliar with the field of biblical studies, it should be said that because the Hebrew corpus abounds in opaque words and phrases, the solution to cruxes has persisted as a prominent area of the field:

academic reputations are still sometimes patiently built on the publication of five-page articles on topics like "A New Solution to a Crux in Habakkuk." Here is a much-discussed crux from the victory psalm at the end of the David story (2 Samuel 22: 36): "Your *'anot* made me many." The noun I have not yet translated already caused confusion in the ancient world—the scribe copying this poem from Samuel in the Book of Psalms as Psalm 18 transformed it into a similar-looking word that means "humility." The modern versions are all at a loss. One translation, assuming the word means "to answer," introduces a circumlocution indicating that God answers His followers. Another, following the "humility" variant, proposes that God lowers Himself to rescue His faithful. The Jewish Publication Society cops out by translating the term as "providence," with no philological warrant, and then adding in a footnote that the meaning is uncertain. But *'anot* means two things—"to answer," and by a semantic skid, "to speak up" or "to call out." (It is used in this sense repeatedly in Job for the introduction of speeches.) If one looks at the poetic context here, the term appears in a small catalogue of powerful *weapons* that God provides to His warriors. This very term occurs in Exodus 32:18 when Joshua, a military man, says to Moses of the Israelites' noisy worship of the golden calf, "Not the sound of crying out [*'anot*] in triumph, / and not the sound of crying out [*'anot*] in defeat. / A sound of crying out [*'anot*] I hear." If one puts this relevant parallel text together with the poetic context of weaponry in 2 Samuel 22, it seems highly likely that the word here means "battle cry," a shout that strikes fear in the heart of the enemy, something like "the sword of the LORD," on the analogy of the battle cry used by Gideon's warriors to terrify the Midianites in Judges 7:20.

The absence of a literary perspective in the training of biblical scholars thus leads to serious deficiencies in the translations they produce, but at least as problematic is the fact that most of them appear to be out of touch with the literary culture of our own times. The contrast with the 1611 translators is painfully evident. We live in an age of specialized bodies of knowledge, a little like special teams in football. If you are laboring in the vineyards of the ancient Near East at Harvard or Johns Hopkins, attending to its languages and to its archaeological terrain, you are not likely to be spending much time reading the novels of Saul Bellow or Ian McEwan or the poetry of W. S. Merwin. There is, then, a double problem: not only do the modern translators lack a clear sense of what happens stylistically in the Bible, but also their notion of English style, its decorums and its expressive possibilities, tends to be rather shaky. The essential point in all this is that the Hebrew Bible by and large exhibits consummate artistry in the language of its narratives and of its poetry, and there must be an answering art in the translation in order to convey what is remarkable about the original.

I encountered a symptomatic instance of this problem when I first began translating the Bible. I had sent a copy of my Genesis to an eminent biblical scholar with whom I had been friendly for many years. He was a superbly intelligent man of impressive erudition. He also had been a member of one of those scholarly committees that produced a new translation of the Bible, something that manifestly influenced his response to my Genesis. Though he tried to be diplomatic when he wrote back to me, it was clear that he thoroughly disliked my translation. One of his principal objections was to my repeated use of "and" at the beginning of sentences and clauses, in keeping with the Hebrew. The English language, he wrote me, could not tolerate the proliferation of "ands" in the manner of biblical Hebrew, and so a rearrangement in translation of the syntax was called for. For all his acuteness, this objection reflected a distinct lack of awareness of what could be done with English literary style. As a literary scholar I had devoted a good deal of work to subtleties of style in English, and my rejoinder to my scholarly friend was that many masters of English prose, in part precisely because of the King James Version, had culti-vated parataxis as a resource of expression. I noted in my re-sponse that Molly Bloom's soliloquy at the end of Joyce's *Ulysses* (which I suspect my friend had never read) uses "and" extrava-gantly again and again in parataxis, and manages to be the greatest piece of extended prose poetry in the English language of the twentieth century.

This clash over the use of "and" reflects what strikes me as a lack of imagination about the possibilities of English style that has been repeatedly evinced by the twentieth-century scholarly translators of the Bible. At least as grave, I think, is their very frequent insensitivity to the apt idiomatic use of the English language. It is somewhat perplexing that this should be the case, for these are, after all, highly educated people from whom one might expect a certain degree of general cultivation. My suspicion is that the problem stems from the specialization of knowledge that leads to a focusing on one area of rather techni-cal expertise and a lack of intimate connection with other cul-tural spheres—precisely what was not true for the King James translators. Though I have no specific biographical information about the modern translators, it seems unlikely that they would have had any serious exposure to the prose of Margaret Atwood or Philip Roth, and, going back a few decades, to the prose of Nabokov, Faulkner, Hemingway, or Virginia Woolf, on the evi-dence of their own use of the English language. Let me offer a few examples.

Genesis 1:16 in my translation—but I will for the moment leave one word untranslated—reads as follows: "And God made the two great lights, the great light for *memshelet* of day and

the small light for *memshelet* of night, and the stars." The Hebrew word left untranslated is a verbal noun derived from the
root that means "to rule," which is usually how it is represented
in the older translations. Several modern versions opt for "to
govern," which is not an altogether grating choice but tries to
have it both ways with two different senses of "govern," the
scientific or legal meaning, "to serve as or constitute a law for,"
and the political meaning, which suggests administration
through vested power. Neither of these senses is more than
loosely appropriate to the meaning intended by the Hebrew
writer. The Jewish Publication Society version is more painfully inept: "God made the two great lights, the greater light
to dominate the day and the lesser light to dominate the night,
and the stars." As readers, we should not be indifferent to the
fact that "dominate" entirely wrecks the beautiful cadence of
the Hebrew. This is something I try to preserve by rendering
the phrases as "dominion of day," "dominion of night," and I
will revisit this choice in my chapter on rhythm. But what is
more troubling about "to dominate" is the manifestly tin ear
to the connotations of the word. "Dominate" is a term appropriate for political contexts—as, for example, in a sentence
such as "The Soviet Union dominated the smaller states of
Eastern Europe"—or for sexual perversion with whip and
boots as accoutrements. It is certainly not what the heavenly
luminaries are said to do to the day and night. One readily
sees that a shaky sense of English leads not merely to stylistic
infelicities but to the misrepresentation of what the biblical
text says.

Perhaps improbably, the translators' ear can be still tinnier.
This is how the JPS people render a line from the Song of Songs
(1:13) that in the Hebrew is both delicately and lusciously
erotic: "My beloved to me is a bag of myrrh / lodged between
my breasts." "Bag" is all wrong for the Hebrew *tsror*—too big,

too bulky—which means "bundle," and in this intimate context of the woman's body, surely "sachet." Even worse, "lodged" is comical: it is a choice dictated by the Hebrew verb, which means "to spend the night," but an object lodged between parts of a body unfortunately suggests something like a chicken-bone lodged in the throat. Contrast Chana and Ariel Bloch's elegant solution, which dispenses with the verb and says with fresh directness, "all night between my breasts."

Here is the Revised English Bible's rendering of Exodus 1:15–16: "The king of Egypt issued instructions to the Hebrew midwives, of whom one was called Shiphrah and the other Puah. 'When you are attending the Hebrew women in childbirth,' he told them, 'check as the child is delivered, if it is a boy, kill him.'" Except for the two names and "king of Egypt" and "midwives," there is nothing in these two sentences that does not betray a palpable lapse of judgment. "Issued instructions" is pure bureaucratese, and a gratuitous explanatory gloss on the Hebrew, which reads simply "said." "Attending in childbirth" is a Victorian circumlocution for the straightforward Hebrew verb *meyaldot*, which means "deliver" (or very literally, a transitive verb meaning "to birth"). "As the child is delivered" is a paraphrastic substitution for "on the birthstool," a concrete element of ancient Near Eastern childbirth, which was done in a kneeling position. "Check" is a modern colloquial transformation of the Hebrew "look," and is really an expression that belongs in such sentences as "Check to see if the water is turned off." Finally, "he told them," inserted in the king's dialogue in between commas, represents nothing whatever in the Hebrew and is merely the misguided notion of the British translators as to how dialogue should be varied or "enlivened" by the insertion of such indications, as in conventional schoolboy fiction. In all these ways, the translation turns a beautiful bit of Hebrew narrative into something both ungainly and banal.

Lapses of judgment of this sort are altogether pervasive in the modern translations, ranging, as we have seen in these two examples, from infelicities to downright misrepresentations of the meanings of the original. There are, to be sure, single verses and even whole sequences of verses where the translations manage to be quite apt, but that is the best one can say of these modern English versions. One final illustration should suffice to make the nature of the problem clear.

In 2 Samuel 3:20–25, Abner, the commander of the Saulide forces that have been engaged in a civil war with David, comes to David in Hebron to sue for peace, promising to bring the northern tribes over to David. This is how the Jewish Publication Society committee chooses to convey in English the report of Abner's departure after he has concluded terms with David to end the civil war: "And David dismissed Abner, who went away unharmed." This very short sentence, which will be significantly repeated and then repeated with a crucial change, exhibits two fatal mistakes in translation. The initial verb, *shaleaḥ*, manifestly means "to send off." The translators may well have realized this, but they seem quite unaware that "to dismiss" has a negative connotation—one dismisses a subordinate—but a powerful general who has come to negotiate a peace treaty is "sent off," perhaps even with a ceremonial flourish. The Revised English Bible shows the same misconception that "dismiss" is an appropriate choice. The New Jerusalem Bible altogether changes the meaning by using "allowed him to go" (was he being retained by force?). The obscuring of the narrative shape of the Hebrew is compounded at the end of the verse by representing *beshalom* as "unharmed" (Revised English Bible, "under safe conduct"; the New Jerusalem Bible, "unmolested"). Now, it is true that the biblical *shalom* does not always mean "peace" and often has the sense of "well-being." However, in the present narrative context—and modern translators seem blind to narrative context—"peace" is the compellingly relevant sense. David and Abner have been at war with each other. Now they have agreed on terms, and David pointedly sends off his recent adversary "in peace." As I have indicated, this entire sentence is repeated by the narrator, once more concluding "in peace," and then again by David's courtiers, who report what has transpired to David's general Joab when he returns from a raid. At this point we get a *fourth* repetition of the sentence, by the angry Joab, who will pursue Abner and murder him. But in his iteration, the end of the sentence is ominously lopped off: "Why did you send him off, and he went, going off?" The vengeful Joab cuts "in peace" out of the end of the sentence and underscores the "going off" by using the conjugated form of the verb immediately followed for emphasis by its infinitive. This very verb, moreover, occasionally occurs as a euphemism for "to die." The haunting and extremely artful effect of the three repetitions and then a fourth with a swerve at the end is entirely eliminated from the modern English versions, which don't even show the repetition. Let me quote these three versions, which embarrassingly speak for themselves: Jewish Publication Society, "Why did you let him go? Now he has gotten away!"; the New English Bible, "How could you let him go and get clear away?"; the Jerusalem Bible, "You let him go away and now he has gone—why?"

This is not merely an issue of infelicity but of translation decisions that obscure or even distort what is conveyed in the Hebrew text. Most of the egregious choices here derive from the misguided impulse to explain everything for the English reader in purportedly crystal-clear terms. Thus, none of the translators is willing to concede that sometimes *shalom* actually means "peace." It is their unswerving conviction that the word always has to have a context-specific meaning and needs to be rendered in English in that light. To say that Abner goes off "unharmed" or "unmolested" is to suggest that there might be a possible intention in David's camp to do him harm, but in this meeting in which Abner proposes to bring all the tribes of Israel under David's rule, there is no intimation that anyone harbors such an intention. And to say that Abner goes off "under safe conduct" implies that he may be traveling with some sort of armed guard provided by David—in which case, how is Joab able to murder him so easily? Translating the Bible well is not just a matter of making it sound good—which is to say, appropriately good for an ancient text structurally and semantically different from our linguistic world—but also representing what actually goes on in the Hebrew literary text faithfully and accurately. And it is worth noting that all these translators exhibit a kind of horror of repetition, egregiously failing to recognize that repetition is an essential element of the sophisticated art of biblical narrative—in this instance brilliantly deployed.

A brief comment is in order about this different linguistic world of the Hebrew writings. In the well-known distinction of the translation theorist Lawrence Venuti between "domesticating" and "foreignizing" translations, I would strongly argue that the latter option is the appropriate one for the Bible (even if it might not be the right course for, say, translating a contemporary French novel). Venuti favors foreignizing on political grounds because he sees it as a line of resistance to the global dominance of the major cultural powers. Such reasoning is obviously not applicable to the Bible, but avoiding the creation of the impression that the Bible was written in English the day before yesterday is important for a different reason: the Hebrew texts were fashioned with a linguistic instrument in many respects quite different from that of modern Western languages and in a cultural setting very different from ours, and I think the differences are worth preserving in a translation that can still be readable, despite its foreign and ancient coloration.

In all this, I clearly want to resist the notion of "dynamic equivalence" that has had some currency in recent Bible translations. The basic idea is to transpose the verbal formulations and idioms of the Bible into different ones that are entirely indigenous to the modern target language. One can see how such a procedure could make the "message" of the Bible more immediately accessible to readers in the many far-flung cultures where it is now read, but it inevitably entails a palpable degree of misrepresentation of the Bible's literary vehicle. Let me cite one brief example from one of the best of the English versions guided by dynamic equivalence, an intermittently evocative 1994 Catholic volume, *The Psalter*, framed for liturgical use, approved by a council of bishops, and announced on its title page as "a faithful and inclusive rendering." Here is what it does with Psalm 36:7: "Your integrity towers like a mountain; / your justice runs deeper than the sea. Lord, you embrace all life." My more literal rendering is: "Your justice like the unending mountains, / Your judgment the great abyss, / man and beast the LORD rescues." I would not object strongly to the first two versets of *The Psalter*'s translation, though "integrity" is a poor choice for the Hebrew *tsedeq* and "towers" and "runs deeper than," in reaching for eloquence, are an embellishment of the original. But "you embrace all life" as a dynamic equivalent of "man and beast the LORD rescues" is a flagrantly sermonic and explanatory substitution for the vivid and perfectly transparent Hebrew phrase.

In arguing for fidelity to the actual configurations of the Hebrew, I may seem to be close to the approach of Martin Buber and Franz Rosenzweig in the German translation that they undertook in the 1920s, completed by Buber in the 1950s long after Rosenzweig's premature death. Although my concern in this book is with English renderings of the Bible, a few words are in order about the Buber-Rosenzweig project because it represents such a radical break with all antecedent translations. They put great stress on the orality of the text and consequently arrange their version typographically in rhythmic units. This is an admirable undertaking (even if one may disagree with some of the typography) because, as I argue in chapter 5, the significant rhythms of the Hebrew have been gravely neglected in all the modern English versions except that of Everett Fox, Buber and Rosenzweig's American emulator. But the more salient radicalism of this German project is its effort to effect what Rosenzweig characterizes as "the excavation of the Hebraic character of the individual word." This is, I would concede, a noble aspiration, but it entails two problematic consequences. Buber and Rosenzweig (less so Fox as he revises) are relentlessly etymological in their treatment of the Hebrew. The result is the introduction of many words that do not really exist in the target language. Thus, instead of *Opfer*, "offering," for the Hebrew *qorban*, they use *Dahrnahung*, "nearbringing," because the Hebrew noun derives from a root that means "to draw near." Instead of "cultic pillar" or "stele" for *matseivah*, a noun that derives from a verb meaning "to stand," they translate *Standmark*, a term that has no general currency in German. The Hebrew word for "altar," *mizbeah*, became, in Fox's initial English equivalent of Buber and Rosenzweig's German, "slaughtersite" because the verbal root of this noun means "to slaughter." (He later thought better of this and revised.) Such choices do considerable violence to the idiomatic integrity of the target language while, as far as we can tell, the ancient Hebrew writers manifest perfect pitch in the idiomatic command of their own language, so there is a serious distortion involved in the procedure.

One wonders, moreover, whether the ancient speakers were always so acutely conscious of etymologies as Buber and Rosenzweig appear to have assumed. Did the Hebrews of the first millennium BCE invariably think of "slaughter" when they heard the word *mizbeaḥ*? The fact that there was a *mizbeaḥ* for incense on which no animal sacrifices were offered argues against this inference. The other problem with this etymologizing translation is that some of the etymologies are rather dubious. Thus, Buber and Rosenzweig assert that *tsedeq*, "justice," actually means "verdict" (*Wahrspruch*) with scant evidence for the claim. Should "Justice, justice you shall pursue" (Deuteronomy 16:20) be understood as "Verdict, verdict you shall pursue"? (Fox, perplexingly, renders this in English as "Equity, equity you are to pursue.") Again, by rather contorted reasoning, Buber and Rosenzweig argue that *'ikavdah*, "I shall be honored," actually means "I shall appear," *ich erscheinege mich*. Making the Hebrew character of the language somehow evident in translation is in itself a worthy goal but not when it generates absurdities.

My complaints have been confined to what one might think of as "establishment" translations—that is, English versions done for the mainstream denominations by authorized committees with scholarly and institutional credentials. There has, however, been a proliferation of translations pitched to various special interests—feminist Bibles, Black English Bibles, colloquial American Bibles. Of the last, the most endearing and perhaps the most popular is a translation by a pastor named Eugene Peterson, which he calls not the Bible or the Holy Bible but *The Message* and which is intended to address contemporary readers in their own vernacular. This version has the Lord tell growing things in Genesis to "green up," and in the Lord's Prayer in the New Testament, the speaker asks God to "keep us alive with three square meals." I don't want to dismiss such efforts because they are manifestly devised to make the Bible speak to specific communities that variously regard it as the word of God and may be seeking a sense of immediate relevance. What must be said, though, is that these amount to free adaptations and sometimes transmutations of the biblical texts that do not exactly qualify as translations, and so they remain beyond the scope of my discussion.

Hebrew prose narratives, as I hope these examples have suggested, manifest great subtlety and complexity in their literary shaping, and the same is abundantly true, in somewhat different ways, for biblical poetry. This artfulness, which cannot be separated from the religious meanings of the texts, sometimes can be conveyed effectively in English; sometimes an English solution can be found that to a degree intimates the stylistic strengths of the original, though imperfectly; and sometimes, alas, the translator must throw up his hands in despair because there seems no workable English equivalent for the stylistic effects of the Hebrew. In the chapters that follow, I will try to isolate five of the principal aspects of style in the Hebrew that I think a translator should aim somehow to reproduce in English. The aspiration may seem quixotic, but even a distant approximation of the literary art of the original is preferable to ignoring it altogether.

CHAPTER TWO

Syntax

LITERARY SYNTAX, THE ORDERING of the words, is bound to differ markedly from one language to another. This makes it difficult and at times altogether unfeasible to transfer syntactic patterns in translation from the source language to the target language. Let me cite one central instance in the Bible. The normal syntactical order in biblical Hebrew is: verb-subject-object. Here is an absolutely typical clause from Genesis 1:12 rendered in the order of the Hebrew words (there are only three, which I indicate with hyphenation): "And-put-forth the-earth grass." It would of course be preposterous—not to say unreadable—to translate in this fashion, and so any English version must use normal English syntax: "And the earth put forth grass." This is not even a compromise but rather a basic procedure of all translations.

And yet, as I indicated in the previous chapter, modern translators of the Bible have globally applied the recognition that adjustments in syntax must be made in the transfer from one language to the other and thus have entirely transformed the underlying syntactic patterns of the Hebrew. One unfortunate consequence is that it makes the Bible sound like a rather undistinguished contemporary text and not like a literary work composed in the Near East initially in the early centuries of the first millennium BCE. But this modernizing of the language also has the grave consequence of obscuring much of the literary artistry of the Bible, especially in the narrative prose. I have already addressed the issue of the erasure of parataxis in the modern translations, but because this is such an essential feature of biblical language, some further comments here are in order.

Biblical Hebrew appears to have lent itself readily to paratactic formulations, but it should hardly surprise us that the writers made an artistic virtue of what might seem to some modern readers a limitation in the way language was ordered. Above, I referred to the stately and imposing cadences realized through parataxis in the Flood story. It should be observed, however, that the procession of parallel clauses linked by "and" serves a variety of artful narrative purposes. Here is one striking instance, Rebekah at the well (Genesis 24:16–20) in my translation, which closely follows the parataxis of the Hebrew:

> And she came down to the spring and filled her jug and came back up. And the servant ran toward her and said, "Pray, let me sip a bit of water from your jug." And she said, "Drink, my lord," and she hurried and lowered her jug onto her hand and let him drink. And she let him drink his fill and said, "For your camels, too, I shall draw water until they drink their fill." And she hurried and emptied her jug into the trough, and she ran again to the well to draw water and drew water for all his camels.

As one might expect, the modern English versions eliminate most of the "ands" and replace the parallel clauses with a variety of participial phrases and subordinate clauses. One lamentable effect is to introduce a set of abrupt interrupted rhythms where the Hebrew has one beautifully uncoiling rhythmic sequence. But much more is lost by the dismantling of parataxis. The Hebrew writer has exploited parataxis to produce a representation of Rebekah our foremother as a kind of heroine of hospitality—a defining virtue of civilized behavior in both the Greek and the Hebrew worlds. She appears here in a blur of activity as the clauses linked by "and" rush us from one act she performs to the next—going down to the well, coming back up, responding to the servant's request, even "hurrying" to take down the jug (it was balanced on her shoulder), and rushing back and forth between the well and the man and his camels, implicitly many times because there are ten camels and each would drink many gallons of water after a long journey through the desert. What is notable is that parataxis can serve rather different, even antithetical, narrative purposes. In the Creation story, it conveys a harmonious choreographed series of cosmogonic speech-acts; in the Flood story, it is the vehicle of high epic dignity in the report of the universal cataclysm; with Rebekah at the well, it gives us a sense of breathtaking speed of action. One might, of course, argue that this is not a "natural" way to organize narrative prose in English, but it seems to me, encouraged by the precedent of the King James Version, that it can work in English, and that adherence to the parataxis of the original brings us closer to the impressive artistry of the Hebrew.

Parataxis is above all a device of narrative concatenation. Instead of stipulating causal relations and so showing how one element in the narrative report qualifies or complicates or is a consequence of another, it marches us steadily from one point to the next in the narrative sequence. Let me offer just one

complementary example (also in my translation) to this one
that we have considered in which parataxis is a vehicle of speed.
In this instance, the context is martial rather than bucolic. Here
is a small segment of Gideon's nighttime attack on the Midianite camp (Judges 7:19–21):

> And Gideon came, and the hundred men who were with him,
> to the edge of the camp, at the beginning of the middle watch—
> they had just posted the watchmen—and they blasted on the
> ram's horns and they broke the pitchers and held the torches
> with their left hand, and their right hand the ram's horn to
> blast on, and called out: "Sword for the LORD and for Gideon!"
> And each one stood in his place all round the camp. And all the
> camp ran off and shouted and fled.

The rush of actions of the surprise attack in the middle of
the night is beautifully conveyed in the Hebrew through the
rapid succession of brief clauses joined by "and"—the charge of
the Israelite raiders into the Midianite camp, the blasting on
the ram's horns, the breaking of the pitchers, the battle cry, the
flight of the terrified Midianite troops. Even the temporal notation about the posting of the watchmen, here presented between dashes because it is not prefixed by an "and," is an independent clause that scarcely interrupts the paratactic
progression. Predictably, the modern English versions compromise this narrative force by substituting participial phrases for
independent clauses or by introducing explanatory "whens"
and "thens" where the Hebrew makes do very effectively with
"and." My own paratactic version may suggest that it is viable
to reproduce much of the Hebrew syntax when it is an essential
vehicle of the Bible's narrative art.

Parataxis is a more or less pervasive feature of ancient Hebrew prose, and as I have tried to show, the biblical writers

often found ways to exploit its expressive advantages. It is also the case, however, that narrative syntax is reshaped in order to serve the particular needs of the narrative, or, rather differently, of the poetry, as the writer intuits them. I would like to focus here on the phenomenon of syntactic inversion. Despite the fixed order of predicate, subject, object explained at the outset of this chapter, biblical Hebrew does lend itself more freely to inversions than modern English. Occasionally that flexibility is tapped to produce telling ambiguities. Thus, in the oracle to Rebekah about the twins she will bear, cast in verse as is oracularly appropriate, she is told, *rav ya'avod tsa'ir*, "the elder shall serve the younger" (Genesis 25:23). But, given the fact that in prose the subject generally follows the verb rather than precedes it, these three Hebrew words could also mean, quite subversively, "the younger shall serve the elder." This ambiguity plays out through the last encounter between Jacob and Esau, when Jacob, though he has secured birthright and blessing, repeatedly addresses Esau as "my lord" and refers to himself as "your servant." The ambiguity of the syntax of the oracle—truly Delphic—alas, resists representation in English.

English readers are, of course, familiar with syntactic inversion, though for the most part in poetry written before the turn to modernism in the early years of the twentieth century. To cite one familiar example, Keats's sonnet "On First Looking Into Chapman's Homer" begins, "Much have I travell'd in the realms of gold," inverting the standard order "I have travell'd much," and the syntactic inversion of the third line is still more prominent, "Round many western islands have I been." The degree of temporal distance from inversion at which we stand may actually be an advantage for Bible translation because the switching of expected word order can give the translation a slightly antique coloration and create some resistance to the unfortunate impression conveyed by modern translations that the Bible was written the day before yesterday. Now, when the object of the verb, at least in prose, generally follows the verb, the decision to put it at the head of the sentence gives it special emphasis. It is what linguists call "fronting." It is, in fact, a maneuver that has not entirely disappeared even now. In the *Star Wars* series, Yoda's repeated flipping of syntax has drawn much commentary, one especially amusing linguistic take on it being Adrienne Lafrance's "An Unusual Way of Speaking, Yoda Has" (*The Atlantic* online, December 18, 2015).

A good deal of syntactic fronting in the Bible occurs in dialogue, perhaps because the often-impassioned speakers are moved to lay strong emphasis on a particular word. When Joseph's brothers return from their first expedition to Egypt and report to their aged father that the man "who is lord of the land" will not agree to see them unless they bring Benjamin with them, Jacob replies, in language that is close to verse, "Me you have bereaved. Joseph is no more and Simeon is no more, and Benjamin you would take! It is I who bear it all" (Genesis 42:36, my translation). The Hebrew of the first sentence manifestly pushes against common usage. The ordinary way to say "You have bereaved me" in biblical Hebrew is by a single word, the verb that means "to bereave," to which is appended a first-person singular accusative suffix, *shikaltuni*. This is not, however, what the writer chooses to do. Instead he breaks out the accusative personal pronoun, *'oti*, "me," and then follows it with the verb, *shikaltem*. This move, I would suggest, is very much part of his characterization of Jacob in his old age. From the moment of Joseph's presumed death, he has been a prima donna of paternal grief. Here, he makes a point of putting himself at the head of his sentence as the long-suffering object of multiple bereavements—and at the end of this little speech, without syntactic inversion, he again paints himself as the unique sufferer. Some modern versions entirely erase this crucial emphasis. Others notice it but substitute a little formal circumlocution such as "It is me" or even "It is always me" (of course, violating formal English grammar). But the emphatic force of *'oti*, "me," is in this fashion diminished, when it can be retained simply by recognizing that literary English still tolerates syntactic inversion. Later, when we consider dialogue, I shall explore more complicated examples of divergences from standard usage in reported speech.

Moses's grand valedictory oration in the Book of Deuteronomy, with its fondness for rhetorical flourishes, does a good deal of fronting of accusative personal pronouns, though to very different ends from those in Jacob's speech. Thus, Moses addresses the assembled Israelites: "But you did the LORD take and He brought you out from the iron's forge, from Egypt, to become for Him a people" (Deuteronomy 4:20). The syntactical maneuver is identical with the one we just considered in Genesis 42:36, but in this case the intention is to arraign the people in a rhetoric of admonition: it was you, and nobody else, whom God saw fit to rescue from Egyptian slavery and embrace as His special people, and so you had better be scrupulously conscious of your covenantal obligations. Without the syntactically inverted "you" at the beginning of the sentence, in keeping with the Hebrew, the force of the admonition is diluted. In similar usages elsewhere in Deuteronomy, Moses refers to himself, or occasionally to Joshua: "Against me, too, the LORD was incensed because of you" (Deuteronomy 1:31). The Hebrew actually puts the monosyllabic *gam*, "too," before "against me," which is also a single monosyllabic word, *bi*. The fronting of the pronoun in this sentence expresses a certain

sense of aggrievement on the part of Moses, who is saying
that he himself has suffered because of the behavior of the
people.

Syntactic inversions often occur in Deuteronomy, and, indeed, throughout the Bible with common nouns as well as with
pronouns, and most of these deserve to be preserved in translation. Thus, immediately after the enunciation of the Ten Commandments, Moses summarizes, "These words did the LORD
speak to your whole assembly at the mountain from the midst
of the fire" (Deuteronomy 5:19). It may be objected that the
natural way to render this in modern English is, "The LORD
spoke these words." The Deuteronomist, however, who has for-
mulated Moses's speech wants to emphasize "these words" by
fronting them. In the Hebrew, the Decalogue is not called the
Ten Commandments but rather the Ten Words. *Devarim*,
"words," is a flexible term and here obviously means something
like "utterances." The writer wants to call attention to the words
or utterances, inscribed on stone, as Moses goes on to say, by
God Himself, as the everlasting covenant between God and
Israel. The "words" clearly need to be at the beginning of the
sentence.

So far, all my examples of syntactic reversals have been from
prose. The phenomenon is somewhat different in poetry. As
one might expect, and as is the case in many other languages,
poetry in the Bible allows a good deal more syntactic flexibility
than does prose. In some instances, the motivation for syntactic
inversion closely resembles what we have just seen in the prose.
A clear illustration is this line and a half from Jeremiah (2:13):
"Me they forsook, / the source of living waters // to hew for
themselves cisterns, broken cisterns / that cannot hold water."
God's sense of outrage at having been abandoned by Israel
when He alone can sustain them in life is emphatically ex-
pressed by setting "Me" at the head of the sentence. The differ-

ent modern versions erase this significant syntactic salience. The rendering of the Jewish Publication Society is characteristic: "They have forsaken Me, the Fount of living waters, / And hewed them out cisterns, broken cisterns, / which cannot even hold water." This "normalization" of syntax turns a strong poetic statement into something more pedestrian. The addition, moreover, of "even" in the concluding verset has no warrant in the Hebrew and is a small token of the way modern translators are not willing to trust the direct expressive force of the Hebrew but feel compelled to introduce explanatory words or phrases.

Poetry, of course, thrives on the tracing of formal patterns—symmetrical, antithetical, repetitive—and these are often inscribed in the rearrangements of syntax. Here is a fairly unexceptional line from a speech by Eliphaz in Job (4:3)—it should be noted that the Job poet for the most part saves the great poetry for Job and puts in the mouths of the three comforters conventional poetry that reflects their conventional morality: "Look, you reproved many, / and slack hands you strengthened." My translation closely follows the syntactic order of the Hebrew, which generates a neat chiasm (A:B::B':A') by reversing the order of object and verb in the second half of the line. The line of poetry in this way gives us verbs indicating Job's formerly moral behavior (as Eliphaz sees it) at the beginning and the end ("reproved," "strengthened") with the objects of the verbs ("many," "slack hands") sandwiched together in the middle of the line. The chiastic pattern, moreover, incorporates a complementary antithesis: Job, when he was still virtuous, both reprimanded the wayward and provided help for those who were failing. Let me hasten to add that form is never entirely coextensive with meaning. I don't think the chiasm here has any deeply significant effect. It is chiefly a formal device for elegantly locking together the two halves of the line, and as I hope my rendering will have shown, it can be conveyed in English without much strain.

Here is a stronger use of chiasm from Psalms (18:43): "I crushed them like dust in the wind / like mud in the streets I ground them." The syntactic inversion here is quite easy to reproduce in English because it involves merely putting the second prepositional phrase before the verb. Needless to say, the modern versions regularize the syntax and eliminate the chiasm. Its expressive power should be evident. The speaker, purportedly David, in celebrating his military triumphs closely brackets together "dust in the wind" and "mud in the streets" at the end of the first verset and the beginning of the second verset, surrounding them with "crushed" at the beginning of the line and "ground" at the end. The tight structure of the chiasm thus conveys the encompassing destructive power of the victor over his enemies, and it should definitely be preserved in translation in order to do justice to the poetry. The penultimate line of this psalm traces a more pacific and formally satisfying chiasm: "therefore I acclaim You among nations, O LORD, / and to Your name I would hymn." Thanksgiving psalms conventionally conclude by deploying precisely these two verbs (and the one rendered as "acclaim" also means "give thanks"). The positioning of the prepositional phrase before the second verb produces a chiasm that underscores the firm assertion of the speaker's praise of the God Who has granted him victory—acclaim:LORD::Your name:hymn.

In the poetry of the Prophets there is a good deal of fronting of nouns that are the object of verbs for the sake of emphasis. Thus Isaiah (1:2): "Sons I have nurtured and raised, / but they rebelled against Me." God, as Isaiah represents the words of the deity, manifestly wants to put "sons" at the very head of His statement. He has treated Israel with tender care as a father would care for his sons, and yet their response has been perverse rebellion. The many English versions that regularize the word order lose this force of emphasis. An extended noun-phrase rather than a single word can equally play a role in expressive syntactic inversion as in verse 11 of the same chapter of Isaiah: "and the blood of bulls and sheep and he-goats / I do not desire." The prophet is railing against people content to offer animal sacrifice in the Temple, though their behavior is morally scandalous, even murderous. By putting the compound object of the verb first, Isaiah evokes a whole panorama of slaughtered beasts and then climatically introduces "I do not desire."

Fronting for the sake of emphasis is also sometimes combined with the tight structures of chiasm. A simple but effective example is this famous verse from Isaiah 2:3: "For from Zion shall teaching come forth / and the LORD's word from Jerusalem." Zion is, of course, a synonym for Jerusalem, and so we have the chiastic "Zion" and "Jerusalem" respectively at the beginning and the end of the poetic line with "teaching" and "the LORD's word" as the two middle terms of the chiasm. But it is also important that the name "Zion" stands forth like a proud banner—and the Hebrew word actually means "marker" or "signal"—at the beginning of the line, an effect achieved by reversing the predictable word order of "teaching shall come forth from Zion."

Let me conclude this consideration of syntactic inversion in poetry and why it is important to preserve in translation with two examples from one of the sublime pinnacles of biblical poetry, the Voice from the Whirlwind in Job. Here is how the Job poet introduces us to the Nile habitat of Behemoth, his mythologized version of the Egyptian hippopotamus: "Underneath the lotus he lies, / in the covert of reeds and marsh. // The lotus hedges him, shades him, / the brook willows stand around him" (40:21–22). With a kind of cinematic deftness, the poet wants first to evoke the waterside setting in which Behemoth lives and then the play of the mighty beast in the water. To this end he sets the prepositional phrase of location, "Underneath the lotus" before the verb, and, having drawn attention to it by this syntactic positioning, he goes on in the next line to speak of the shade of the lotus and the surround of brook willows. Finally, to go back from zoa-mythology to zoology proper, here is how the Job poet represents the explosive birth-process of the gazelle (39:3): "They crouch, with their babes they burst forth, / their young they push out to the world." I have exercised a minor liberty by rendering the verb that means "to send out" as "push out to the world," a choice that seems to me justified by the virtual violence of the unusual verb used for birthing, "burst forth," or, more literally, "split open." That is, in the vision of the Job poet, power or even violence is an intrinsic element of the natural realm, and it is manifested even in the act of procreation. In regard to syntax, both "babes" and "young" are inserted before the verbs of which they are the object (in the Hebrew, "babes" is the direct object of "burst forth," and "with" has been added in the translation for the sake of intelligibility in English). The sharp focus is on the offspring. They are the product of the teeming fertility of the creatures of nature, and in the next line of the poem, they will be seen growing big in the wild.

In all these instances, the syntactic suppleness of biblical poetry and its use for expressive ends are vividly evident. Regrettably, the syntactic contours of the poetry have generally been ignored by the modern English translators. It is, I would argue, actually easier to reproduce syntactic inversions and deviations in translating poetry than in prose because we are culturally conditioned to assume that the order of words in poetry can be reconfigured in ways we would not expect it to be in prose. But, to return now to prose narrative, I would like to consider how the purposeful articulation of syntactic chains helps to shape the stories and make them compelling. The artful deployment of syntax is by no means restricted to reversals of common word order: it often is visible simply in the carefully chosen sequence of items, which, again, is frequently overlooked by the modern translators.

One riveting instance, at the beginning of the story of the Binding of Isaac, occurs in God's reported speech to Abraham (Genesis 22:2): "Take, pray, your son, your only one, whom you love, Isaac." Rashi, picking up a cue from the Midrash, beautifully observes the significance of the order of the terms in an invented dialogue: "'Your son.' He said to Him, 'I have two sons.' He said to him, 'Your only one.' He said to him, 'This one is an only one to his mother, and the other is an only one to his mother.' He said to him, 'Whom you love.' He said to Him, 'I love both of them.' He said to him, 'Isaac.' And why did He not reveal it to him from the start? In order not to suddenly confound him." A superficial reading of the story might encourage the inference that Abraham, who registers no response in the text to God's terrible command, is entirely passive in his obedience. The sequence of words in God's speech, as Rashi finely notes, points to an undercurrent of tension in God's obedient servant. It is distressing that the modern English translators fail to see the significance of the sequence and so reorder it: "Take your son, your favored one, Isaac, whom you love"; "Take your son, your one and only one, Isaac, whom you love"; "Take your son, your only son, your beloved Isaac." It is painfully clear that each of these versions aims to make the Hebrew sound a lot more like "natural" modern English usage and also seeks to make it somehow more compact. The lamentable result is to erase an important effect inscribed in the word order of the Hebrew.

Biblical narrative incorporates many brief anticipations of free indirect discourse—that is, the intertwining of the point of view of the narrator and of the character, a technique that much later would become central in the novel. The common marker of the slide of the narrator's perspective into that of the character is the so-called presentative, *hineh*, an approximate equivalent of the French *voici* or *voilà* (usually "lo" in the King James Version and "look" in my translation). Here is the fugitive Jacob arriving at a well in the Mesopotamian countryside from which his family originally came (Genesis 29:2): "And he saw and, look, there was a well in the field, and, look, three flocks of sheep were lying beside it, for from that well they would water the flocks, and the stone was big on the mouth of the well." The first three words here (only a single word in the Hebrew) are the narrator's report of what Jacob is doing. With the transitional marker of "and, look," we move behind the eyes that see the well, and, then, with a second "and, look," make out the flocks of sheep by the well. It is not clear whether the clause, "for from that well they would water the flocks" is the narrator's explanation or Jacob's inference after he sees both the well and the flocks, but such ambiguity is one of the hallmarks of free indirect discourse. The relentlessly normalizing modern versions variously convert the last clause of this sentence into a prosaic statement of fact (e.g., "there was a large stone on the mouth of the well."). The Hebrew, however, remains faithful to Jacob's visual—and perhaps also emotional—perspective. It says, as I have literally represented it in English, "and the stone was big on the mouth of the well." The bigness of the stone is what immediately catches Jacob's eye. Aware that it will be necessary to roll away the stone in order to water the waiting flocks, he may already be sizing it up, gauging whether he has the strength to remove it. All this may seem a small difference—after all, in all the versions we still get the general idea that Jacob sees the well, the flocks, and the stone—but an accumulation of small differences turns a vividly imagined narrative into a more inert one.

Let us consider how the order of terms seen from the perspective of the characters dramatically realizes the discovery of an assassination. In the third chapter of Judges, the Benjaminite warrior Ehud stabs to death Eglon, the Moabite king to whom his people had been subjugated, and then slips out through some rear entrance (the reference is obscure) of the king's upper chamber where the killing took place. Here is the crucial report (verses 24–25): "He had just come out, when Eglon's courtiers came and saw and, look, the doors of the upper chamber were locked. And they said, 'He must be relieving himself in the cool chamber.' And they waited a long time, and, look, no one was opening the doors of the upper chamber. And they took the key and opened them, and, look, their master was fallen to the ground, dead." As in the passage from Genesis 29, the move into the point of view of the character (here, a collective) is prefaced by the verb "saw." In this case there is a triple repetition of "and, look," emphasizing not only the visual perspective of the courtiers but also the fact that what they see is unanticipated (*hineh* often points to a *surprising* perception): they don't expect the doors of the king's chamber to be locked, and they explain that fact comically because they detect an unpleasant odor from within, of course, not knowing that Eglon's anal sphincter was released as he was stabbed; then they are baffled by the long time in which the doors remain locked. After the third "and, look," the order of the terms is strategically imagined: first they see their master, also taking in the incongruous fact that he is lying on the ground; then, at the very end of the syntactic chain, they realize that he is "dead." It requires not the slightest reconfiguration of modern English syntax to reproduce this dramatic effect, but, unaccountably, the modern English versions choose to "improve" on the Hebrew by translating it as "lying dead on the floor" or some equivalent.

Sometimes the report of the character's viewpoint is deliberately interrupted by an observation that comes entirely from the narrator, and in such cases, too, the order of observations is important and has to be maintained in translation. Here is Abraham's servant first seeing Rebekah as she approaches the well to draw water (Genesis 24:15–16): "He had barely finished speaking when, look, Rebekah was coming out, who was born to Bethuel the son of Milcah, the wife of Nahor, Abraham's brother, with her jug on her shoulder. And the young woman was comely to look at, a virgin, no man had known her." The order of items is so clear that one would think no translator would scramble it, and, in fact, several of the modern versions get it right, though they chop up the flow of the first long sentence and also introduce some syntactic subordination. The Revised English Bible, however, sees fit to lift the notation of Rebekah's pedigree out of its place in the sequence and set it out as an independent sentence after the jug on the shoulder— another reflection of the modern impulse to improve Scripture by rearranging it. But why is the sequence as it stands in the Hebrew important? The servant, just having finished his prayer for an eligible young woman to appear and provide water both for him and his camels, raises his eyes and "look" (*hineh*), there is a young woman, though of course he can have no knowledge of her name and lineage. For this information, the narrator must immediately intervene because he wants to make it perfectly clear to his audience from the outset that Rebekah is Abraham's kin and hence an appropriate match for Isaac. The first thing caught by the servant's eye is the jug on the girl's shoulder—a crucial item because he has just stipulated the necessary condition of the girl's providing water. Then he sees that she is beautiful, and to her attractiveness as a potential bride for Isaac, the narrator, intervening a second time, adds the important fact that she is unquestionably a virgin. The order of terms, it should be evident, has been carefully arranged by the writer, and it behooves the translator to reproduce that order scrupulously.

Let me conclude by noting that the order of items in a simple syntactic chain is also sometimes quite essential in reported speech. I shall offer a single very concise example, one which is subtle for all its seeming simplicity. When Esau returns empty-handed from the hunt to find Jacob by his pot of lentil stew and tells his brother that he thinks he is about to die of hunger, Jacob responds in these words, in this order: "Sell now your birthright to me" (Genesis 25:31). These are the very first words of dialogue assigned to Jacob in the narrative, and it is worth keeping in mind that as a general principle in biblical narrative a character's first words are used to lay out the characterization of that figure. Jacob, of course, will turn out to be a shrewd dealer and a rather calculating man—he even bargains with God during the dream-epiphany at Bethel. To the desperate Esau's plea for a portion of lentil stew, he responds with only six words (in the Hebrew, four words), each in its carefully or-dered place in the sequence. None of the English translations I have looked at respects this strategic order, not even the King James Version. Let me unpack the way the order works. First Jacob pronounces the imperative verb: "sell." Then he stipu-lates when the sale is to be consummated—not tomorrow or next week but "now." Then, he introduces the extremely fraught object of the sale, which he has held back from Esau until this penultimate moment in his brief speech: "the birthright"; and, finally, at the very end of the chain, virtually lying in wait to snap shut like a trap on the seller, the person to whom the birthright is to be conveyed: "to me." In this fashion, the order in which four Hebrew words are placed brilliantly effects an initial characterization of Jacob as a calculating self-interested deal-maker, in utter contrast to his twin brother, who here is all impatient appetite, impulsivity, and inarticulateness. It takes almost no effort to reproduce this significant sequence of words in English, but the twentieth-century translators have failed to do so because they simply have not noticed the highly artful ordering of the Hebrew.

Biblical narrative is famously laconic. What this means in regard to its literary art is that individual words and phrases, and the order in which they occur, have a salience they would not have if they were submerged in the proliferation of the sheer numbers of words of a novel. This is an aspect of ancient Hebrew narrative to which we will return when we go on to consider the need to reflect the exacting nature of biblical word choice in translation. But I hope I have shown in regard to the ordering of words that if an English version makes no attempt to mirror the order of the original, the force and subtlety of the Hebrew texts are often blunted and sometimes altogether obscured. There are, of course, instances in which literary effects are achieved through the manipulation of syntax in the original that cannot be reproduced in translation because acceptable English usage will not permit it. More often, though, English syntax can be stretched to achieve much the same literary end observable in the Hebrew, and in many cases, such as the ones considered in the last section of this chapter, no stretch at all is required. The cardinal principle is that a translator has to see the literary shape of the Hebrew in fine detail, or the translation will turn it into something cruder, or more banal, than the original text is in fact. Stylistically, the Bible is very often quite different from the models of literary style to which we are habituated from modern literature, but, with scrupulous attention to the artful workings of the Hebrew, it is frequently possible to create reasonable equivalents in translation that are readable as literary English.

CHAPTER THREE

Word Choice

SINGLE WORDS ARE, of course, important in any original literary work because it is through words that the reality of the fictional or poetic world is shaped. This is not the case for run-of-the-mill writing because its reliance on stereotypical language frequently makes one word or a phrase readily interchangeable with several others. In the novel, where vast quantities of words have often been produced at breakneck speed, as in the signal instances of Dickens and Balzac, individual words might seem to carry less weight, though this is truer for Balzac (sometimes an indifferent stylist) than for Dickens, who, even while composing rapidly for serial publication, had an uncanny intuition for hitting on the inventively right—and sometimes quite surprising—word. It is also well to keep in mind the so-called art-novel, pioneered by Flaubert, which involves painstaking refinement through revision, focused on finding in every formulation *le mot juste*, the exactly appropriate word. But, as I observed earlier, the sheer abundance of words in the novel sets it off from biblical narrative. You can translate a novel by Flaubert into English, or one by Henry James into French, and from time to time fumble in conveying the precision or elegance of a particular word choice without seriously damaging the overall effect of the narrative. The biblical writers, on the other hand, are so sparing in their use of language that the choice of single words is constantly telling, and if the translator gets one word wrong, it may throw an episode off-balance or even altogether misrepresent it. I do not mean to exaggerate the stylistic achievement of narrative art in the Bible. There are certainly stretches of boilerplate language in the Bible, perhaps especially in some of the later books such as Ezra-Nehemiah, Daniel, and Chronicles. By and large, though, the great stretch of narratives from Genesis through Kings, to which one may add Ruth, Jonah, Ecclesiastes, and Esther, manifest a subtlety and a sense of strategic appropriateness in the choice of words that is—or certainly should be—a repeated challenge to the translator. Let us consider two general categories of word choice in which English translations have done a less than adequate job in handling this challenge.

Inaccuracies

The modern philological study of the Bible has devoted a formidable amount of energy to getting the meanings of biblical terms exactly right. I would be the first to admit that in far too many cases this proves to be impossible. If a word appears only once or twice in the biblical corpus, if its verbal root is opaque or ambiguous, if cognates proposed from other ancient Semitic languages seem dubious, we may be able to do no more than guess at its meaning on the basis of context. In all intellectual honesty, we will never know biblical Hebrew with the sureness that its native speakers enjoyed. That being said, there has certainly been progress in the accurate understanding of biblical Hebrew through the twentieth century to the present that is visible in the modern translations by committee to which I have objected on other grounds. It is nevertheless surprising that the modern versions, even if they do not make the sort of egregious errors one encounters in the King James Bible, are marred by misunderstandings of the Hebrew.

I have already noted one striking instance, where the hard edge of armor in both the Samson story and the battlefield scene between Joab and Asahel is turned into soft cloth—tunics, garments, even belts—by inattention to the relevant narrative context and invocation of the wrong etymology. Such errors unfortunately abound, sometimes missing a nuance, sometimes the point of the story. Let me offer a few examples. When God is about to reveal the Ten Commandments to Moses (Exodus 19:9), every translation I have looked at represents Him coming in a "thick cloud" or "dense cloud." The Hebrew actually exhibits a grand stylistic flourish that is rather different. The word for "thick" is 'aveh, but a different word is used here, 'av, which means "cloud," immediately followed by 'anan, another word that means "cloud." (A rough equivalent in English of the literal effect would be "the thunderhead of the cloud.") Now, for some reason biblical philologists have failed to notice that when two synonyms are joined together in what is called the construct state (the X of Y, as in "the house of David"), the effect is an intensification or an emphatic heightening. There are dozens of such instances in the biblical corpus, a memorable one occurring a little earlier in Exodus (10:22)—hoshekh 'afeilah, literally, "darkness of darkness," which has to mean something like "pitch-dark." The 'av he'anan, then in Exodus 19:9 is not simply a "thick cloud," which all of us have seen on a rainy day, but a virtually mythological super-cloud, the appropriate vehicle for God to come down in to deliver His ten imperative utterances, and so I propose rendering it as "the utmost cloud." The mistaken construction of 'av as "thick" does not entirely alter the moment, but it takes away something of its high solemnity.

It is also odd that the modern translators in all their zeal to put aside the precedent of the King James Version and redo everything from the ground up, continue to perpetuate some of the errors of the 1611 translation. Every biblical scholar knows that *nefesh* means "breath," "life-breath," "life," "essential self," and sometimes, by metonymy, "throat," "neck," and even "appetite," yet the number of times it is still rendered as "soul" in the modern versions is disconcerting. It is as if the translators felt that you can't really have a Bible without "soul." But it is always a misleading English equivalent because there is no biblical notion of the soul, and the several concretely physical meanings I have just listed reflect a rather different conception of the living human body.

There are even instances in which the moderns slide into error where the King James Version got it right. I mentioned earlier that the 1611 translators correctly understood that *ḥalitsah* in the Joab-Asahel encounter meant "armor," not "tunic." A still more striking modern misconstruction is Song of Songs 4:1: "Your eyes are doves / through the screen of your tresses." The several modern versions represent the final noun of this line as "veil." Ariel Bloch, in his acute commentary on the Song, persuasively observes that the form of the noun *tsamah* is one generally reserved for body parts; that when this word occurs in Isaiah 47:2, it is the object of a verb that means "to lay bare," never "to remove" (a garment); and that the line is part of a vertical celebration of the beauty of the beloved's body, not of her garments. Where the Hebrew poet wrote "tresses" (King James Version, "locks"), the modern translators cast a chaste veil over the young women's lovely eyes, which in fact are sexily peeking out from her lustrous dark hair that partly covers them.

Here is an instance in which translators, riding the momentum of antecedent versions, avert their gaze from both archaeological and etymological evidence. When Pharoah, making Joseph his viceroy, has him clothed in regal raiment, he puts a golden *ravid* around Joseph's neck. The noun does not appear elsewhere. All the English versions, from Tyndale to the King James Version to the moderns, represent this as a chain. But we have abundant visual depictions of Egyptian royalty in paintings and sculpture, and they are not wearing chains, an adornment more suited to Venetian doges or nobles in the court of Henry VIII. What they do sometimes wear is a kind of ornate gold chestplate that comes down over the neck and between the shoulders. The verbal stem of *ravid* (*r-b-d*), moreover, is probably related to *rapad*, which means to cushion, to overlay, to pave. In modern Hebrew the root was suitably taken up as the verb meaning "to upholster." Clearly, what is called for here is an ornament more substantial than "chain." My own version uses "collar," with the idea that there are ornamental collars which don't just go around the neck but cover the upper chest. This is a fairly minor point, but reducing the golden *ravid* to a chain makes Joseph's elevation to higher office just a little less grand, and a little less Egyptian.

Sometimes the translation errors occur not because the translators have misunderstood the Hebrew but because they are unwilling to convey what it actually means, their own imagination being more timid than that of the ancient writer. Thus, in Genesis 21:15, after Hagar has been driven out into the desert with her child Ishmael and the water in her waterskin is exhausted, in the sundry modern versions she "lays," "puts," "abandons" her son under one of the bushes and goes off at a distance so that she will not have to see the child dying. The King James Version is a little better than all of these, having her "thrust" the boy under one of the bushes. But the Hebrew verb *hishlikh* means only one thing, "to fling." It is the very verb Pharoah uses when he says, "Every boy that is born you shall fling into the Nile" (Exodus 1:22). What this jolting verb suggests is the terrible violence of Hagar's emotions at this moment of crisis. She is convinced that her only son is on the point of dying, and so in a paroxysm of maternal despair, she does not set him down under a bush but flings him down, and then runs off. The startling effect of this moment is blunted by the translators' choice of these verbs that in effect bowdlerize it.

Here is another instance in which the translators' command of Hebrew should have enabled them to know better, but a reticence about recognizing the boldness of the original led them astray. The most common word for "God" in the Hebrew, *'elohim*, famously has a plural ending but is treated grammatically as a singular, whether because it is a linguistic fossil harking back to a period when everyone spoke of "the gods" or because it is something like a plural of majesty (if in fact that actually existed in biblical Hebrew). All biblical scholars are aware that when the noun is treated grammatically as a plural it refers to "the gods," as in Aaron's words about the golden calf. "These are your gods, O Israel, who brought you up from the land of Egypt" (Exodus 32:4). But when Abraham tells Abimelech how he became a wanderer (Genesis 20:13), all the English versions have "God" impose this fate on him despite the fact that here *'elohim* is unambiguously the subject of a plural verb, so that it must be rendered, "When the gods made me a wanderer from my father's house." This is a small but vivid instance of the liveliness of the dialogue in the Bible, a topic we shall take up in another chapter. Abraham is speaking with a polytheist, and he wants to address him in language entirely accessible to his interlocutor. In fact, his choice of words might well reflect an ancient "manner of speaking"—the gods, *'elohim*, which is to say, circumstances, fate, my destiny, made me wander from my father's house. What Abraham clearly does *not* want to hint at in his words to Abimelech is that the one God, as part of a covenantal promise, commanded him to leave his father's house. The piquancy of the patriarch's adjusting his terms to the ear of a pagan monarch is altogether lost by the translations that make him out to be an impeccable monotheist in all his dealings.

I alluded above to the unfortunate continuation of a negative legacy of the King James Version in its dilution of the strong concreteness of the Hebrew, sometimes through the substitution of a more pallid English term for the counterpart in the Hebrew, sometimes through the insertion of a theologically fraught term where none is present in the Hebrew (for example, in Psalms "tabernacle" where the Hebrew uses a simple agricultural term, "shelter"). The crucial case in point is the representation of God in unabashedly anthropomorphic terms, especially in the J narrative in Genesis but sometimes also elsewhere. Some of this no translation can obscure: God goes walking in the Garden in the evening breeze (*ruaḥ hayom*). He appears before Abraham's tent with two accompanying celestial messengers looking altogether like an ordinary wayfarer, and the hospitable Abraham hastens to lay out a sumptuous meal for all three. Concluding the instructions for observing the sabbath in Exodus 31:17, this is what is said of God's own resting on the seventh day: ". . . six days did the LORD make heaven and earth and on the seventh day He ceased and *wayinafash.*" What does this verb at the end of the sentence mean? Most English versions, following the King James translators, render it as "was refreshed" (did He have a cool drink?). Others simply understand it to mean "rested." The Catholic New Jerusalem Bible gets halfway to accuracy by rendering it as "drew breath." Now, the verb used here transparently derives from *nefesh*, "breath" and is also semantically related, in a reversal of the second and third consonants, to *nashaf*, "to pant" or "to breathe hard." In Exodus 23:12 it is used for the cessation from hard labor of the bondsmen and the sojourner. Even more tellingly, in its other occurrence, 2 Samuel 16:14, it is used for David and his troops who have fled from Absalom's forces and, exhausted, stop for what today we would call a breather. All this evidence argues strongly that the phrase in Exodus 31:17 should be translated, "He ceased and caught His breath." Clearly, the God of Aquinas and Maimonides and of modern churches and synagogues is never thought to be out of breath, but the Hebrew writer is not likely to have had much trouble imagining Him that way. God had labored strenuously for six days to bring the heavens and the earth and all that is in them into existence, and now on the seventh day, He catches His breath and rests, a model that the toiling Israelites are enjoined to emulate each week. The misrepresentation of *wayinafash* in the extant English versions reflects a kind of airbrushing of the Hebrew, which deserves to be conveyed in all its palpable physicality.

Diction

There are, then, as I hope I have shown, many more errors in the various English versions of the Bible than one might expect. Some of these reflect lapses in the philological grasp of the Hebrew; many more, as the concluding group of examples in the section above illustrates, are the consequence of a kind of timidity or lack of imagination in seeing what the Hebrew writers are actually doing. But far more pervasive in the modern translations—and in this respect there is a real contrast with the more apt King James Version—is the failure to create an appropriate kind of diction for rendering the Bible in English.

Broadly, there are three general levels of diction manifested in the ancient Hebrew: a specialized poetic diction for the poems that was probably somewhat archaic even in its own time; a plain middle diction for the narratives, about which I will have more to say presently; and a language used for the dialogues (an essential component of biblical narrative) that manages to be proper literary Hebrew, with only limited exceptions, while incorporating certain gestures toward the colloquial. The language of the dialogues will be taken up in detail in a separate chapter.

It is remarkable—and, indeed, anomalous—that the narrative literature of ancient Israel was cast in prose, in contrast to the practice of other early cultures. Various contested explanations have been proposed for this choice, but these lie beyond the scope of our considerations of translation. What one can safely say is that the use of prose was obviously connected with the presence of literacy in this culture, as opposed to Homer's world, which did not know writing. Freed from the constraints of oral-formulaic composition in metrical lines, the Hebrew writers enjoyed an impressive flexibility in how they could shape language.

In regard to the language of the biblical poems, the greatest challenge is how to convey in English something of its terrific—and often quite significant—rhythmic compactness, but that is an issue I shall consider in the chapter on rhythm. Translating the poems also often entails thorny issues of understanding what the words mean because the poets frequently used rare terms, and in keeping with the difficulty of the language, the ancient scribes often scrambled the transmission of words they themselves found unfamiliar. As to our present concern with diction, the modern versions have by and large exerted a visible effort to make the language of the poetry sound poetic and perhaps a little antique. This is an aim that has to be pursued with some caution because a translator obviously needs to avoid such coyly archaic terms as "anent" and "forsooth," and, fortunately, there is little evidence of them in the modern versions. What one does find in recent English translations of biblical poetry is abundant minor slips out of poetic diction into locutions that belong in some other kind of text and thus produce local dissonances. The Song of Deborah, Judges 5, is probably the oldest extended poem in the Hebrew Bible. Its splendidly archaic language sounds virtually epic, and the parallelism of its lines abounds in incremental repetition, a feature of the oldest Hebrew poems, and resonant sound play. The different modern versions do strive to suggest these qualities in English, but they are marred by the introduction of such terms as "commemorate," "consorted with," "inhabitants," "orbits," "split into factions," and, beyond such stiffly formal language, an occasional turn into such conversational phrases as "a couple of." None of these sounds as though it belongs in a martial poem composed more than three centuries before Homer, around 1100 BCE.

Let me cite just one brief instance in which all the translations, in varying ways, miss representing the poetic diction of the Hebrew. The onset of the Flood, Genesis 7:12, is marked with an epic flourish by a single line of poetry: "All the well-springs of the great deep burst / and the *'arubot* of the heavens were opened." The untranslated noun has been clearly understood for many centuries, quite correctly, to mean "windows." (Rashi offers an equivalent in the language he spoke, Old French—*fenestra*.) Some modern translators simply use "windows." Others, unpardonably, try to improve the Hebrew by substituting their own metaphor, "floodgates" or "sluices," for the biblical one. Now, while *'arubot* certainly means "windows," it is by no means the ordinary term for a window. That would be *ḥalon*, which occurs dozens of times in the biblical corpus while *'arubah*, by contrast, appears only nine times, and in all but two cases in poetic texts. The compelling inference is that it reflects specialized poetic diction and was quite possibly somewhat archaic in its own era—a close cognate appears in Ugaritic poetry, which antedates the earliest biblical texts perhaps by three or four centuries. With all this in mind, I have proposed rendering it as "casements," a word for windows one finds in Keats and in Shakespeare but not in modern usage except in the technical sense of a window opening outward on hinges that are set along a vertical edge.

The misjudgments of translators in rendering biblical poetry are no more than occasional flies in a generally smooth ointment. The real problems are visible in the translation of the narrative prose. It might seem that it should be relatively easy to translate biblical prose. It works with a rather limited vocabulary—quite deliberately, as I argued earlier—and it does not pose problems in regard to the ordering of language (especially if one respects its configurations of syntax, as I proposed in the previous chapter). The linguistic register of the narrative prose is what I have characterized as a middle diction. It consistently excludes poetic terms and at the same time does not seem to reflect much in the way of vernacular usage. Indeed, some analysts have contended that there was an ancient vernacular with somewhat different words for a good many everyday actions and objects that subsequently surfaced in rabbinic Hebrew, a stratum of the language that exhibits abundant lexical divergences from its biblical predecessor. The language of the narratives possesses an eloquent dignity of simplicity— one might recall the striking use of the primary verbs *was* and *went* in the Flood story that we considered earlier. An adequate translation of the narrative prose must above all respect its directness and simplicity. The impulse of the modern translators to effect in English what they imagine as an improvement of the original often amounts to a lamentable tampering with it.

Here, for example, are two verses from the Jewish Publication Society translation of the story of the rape of Tamar, the first a rearrangement of the Hebrew that entirely effaces a brilliant literary effect and the second a misguided elevation of its primary diction. When Amnon, lusting after his half-sister Tamar, has succeeded in luring her into his bedchamber on the pretext of having her bring him food on his purported sickbed, this is how the action is represented in the JPS version: "but Amnon refused to eat and ordered everyone to withdraw" (2 Samuel 13:9). What the reader of this translation could not guess is that the Hebrew actually conveys this as *dialogue*: "And Amnon said, 'Clear out everyone around me.'" This bit of dialogue is actually a pointed allusion to the Joseph story: when Joseph is about to reveal his true identity to his brothers (Genesis 45:1), he speaks exactly these words. The quoted dialogue, in turn, is the first of three allusions to the Joseph story in 2 Samuel 13, following a reverse order to the occurrences of the alluded-to texts in Genesis: first, here, Joseph's words to his brothers, which appear near the end of his story; then the sexually imperative words of Potiphar's wife, here readdressed by Amnon to Tamar; and, finally, the ornamented tunic (or "coat of many colors"), which appears at the beginning of the Joseph story and in the dire aftermath of Tamar's being raped by her brother. In the Joseph story, "Clear out everyone around me" is the prelude to the moving reconciliation between brother and brothers. Here, in a bitterly ironic reversal, it is the prelude to a brother's sexual assault on his sister that will fatally set brother against brother. This powerful point is, of course, invisible in the JPS version. What could have led them to tamper with the text and suppress this crucial bit of dialogue? Their intervention is clearly dictated by a misguided notion that the narrative should be made to move along more "efficiently": entirely failing to see the allusion, the translators substitute for the fraught dialogue the bland "Amnon . . . ordered everyone to withdraw."

After the rape, as Amnon prepares to brutally drive out the sister he has violated, we are told of him, in the JPS version, "Then Amnon felt a very great loathing for her; indeed, his loathing for her was greater than the passion he had felt for her" (2 Samuel 13:15). Now, biblical Hebrew does have a few terms that might be approximate equivalents of "loathing" and "passion"—one might find them especially in the poetry of the Prophets—but, in keeping with the convention of lexical restriction, they would never be used in narrative prose. What the Hebrew actually says is: "And Amnon hated her with a very great hatred, for greater was the hatred with which he hated her than the love with which he had loved her." There is, of course, no hint of the rhetorical "indeed," a small annoyance in the JPS rendering of this verse, but the essential issue is that the Hebrew writer has chosen to use the primary terms "love" and "hate" and not any context-bound explanatory terms. This plain diction helps realize what I have called the dignity of the biblical mode of storytelling, and it also raises thematic questions that "passion" and "loathing" blur. The early rabbis understood the point of the primary terms perfectly well. They cited the love between David and Jonathan as "love that is not dependent on physical gratification [literally, 'a thing']" and Amnon's love for Tamar as "love that is dependent on physical gratification." Amnon's desire for his sister is of course imperious lust, but the writer's use of the primary word "love" suggests that the demarcation between love and lust could be ambiguous: perhaps Amnon thought he loved his sister in wanting her body; having consummated his desire, he feels revulsion, possibly because he resents her for having drawn him through her beauty to commit an act that may now gravely compromise him with their father or with her full brother Absalom (who in fact will subsequently have him killed). It makes perfect sense for this sudden revulsion to be named "hatred" in symmetrical antithesis to the preceding "love." It should be evident that the restricted vocabulary of biblical narrative is a resource, not a limitation, and that translators should not obscure the ways in which this resource is deployed.

Such violations of the beautiful plain diction of the Hebrew narrative swarm through all the modern versions because the translators are unwilling to trust the Hebrew and repeatedly feel the need to explain it or in some way embellish it. One final, extended example should suffice to conclude this consideration and to illustrate that there is a better way for the translator to go. Let us look at the rendering of the episode of Joseph and Potiphar's wife in the Revised English Bible, first published in 1961 and thus contemporary with the versions of the other major denominations and carried out by a large team of eminent British biblical scholars (the citations are from Genesis 39:6–15). In the language of this version, the story of female desire and male resistance begins as follows: "Now Joseph was handsome in both face and figure, and after a time his master's wife became infatuated with him. 'Come, make love to me,' she said." This amounts to an interpretive riff on the Hebrew, which actually says, "his master's wife raised her eyes to Joseph and said, 'Lie with me.'" There is no hint of "infatuation" in the original. If there were an equivalent in biblical Hebrew for that verb, which is not the case, it would certainly have been excluded as the wrong kind of diction for narrative. But it is also wrong for what it implies in English. A teenage girl might be infatuated with a movie star, but this married—and perhaps mature—woman lusts after the beautiful young man, probably only in his early twenties if one recalls that he was seventeen when he was sold into slavery. The woman's raising her eyes to look at the gorgeous young man disappears here and with it the essential point that it is the sight of Joseph's beauty that inflames her desire. The translational disaster of this single verse does not stop here: instead of the direct, even brusque, "Lie with me," we are given a softer expression that belongs to sex in the modern world, "Make love to me." It should be noted that verbs for sexual intercourse are a particular challenge for the translator. The biblical writers most commonly use one of three ordinary verbs in a sexual sense: "to lie with," "to know," and "to come into." Translators would be wise to hew closely to the literal equivalents of these three. "To make love" is manifestly off-key either in a biblical narrative or any other kind of biblical text. Elsewhere, in the modern versions, one encounters a variety of locutions for the act of sex that are variously euphemistic, stiffly formal, or vaguely medical or legalistic—"to be intimate with," "to have intercourse with," "to cohabit with"—and painfully violate the stylistic decorum of the Hebrew.

In our text, the British translators stumble onward: "But Joseph refused. 'Think of my master,' he said: 'he leaves the management of the whole house to me; he has trusted me with all that he has. I am as important in this house as he is, and he has withheld nothing from me except you, because you are his wife.'" "Think of my master" is another modernizing interpretive intervention that reflects nothing in the Hebrew, which says, "Look, my master has given no thought with me here to what is in the house, and all that he has he has placed in my hands." What is especially egregious is that the translators have eliminated the concrete idiom "place in my hands" (the Hebrew uses a singular, "my hand"), a phrase that recurs several times from the beginning of the chapter onward and that will be pointedly turned around when Joseph leaves his garment that

Potiphar's wife has seized "in her hand," which in her lying version of the encounter she will change into "he left his garment by me," hiding the truth that she tore the garment off his back. Joseph, in the Hebrew, says "He is not greater in this house than I," but here the primary term "great" (*gadol*) is switched to "important," and, worse, a modern administrative phrase, "leaves the management" displaces "he has placed in my hands."

The distortions of the translation multiply as we approach the attempted sexual assault. "Though she kept on at Joseph day after day, he refused to lie with her or be in her company." The phrase "kept on at" is an interpretive substitution for the plain Hebrew phrase, "And she spoke to Joseph day after day." Though one might be grateful that the translators here give us "lie with" instead of "make love to," the next phrase, "be in his company" is a truly regrettable rendering of the simple phrase in the original, "to be with." The idiom almost makes it sound as though she had something like dating in mind. The Hebrew is an obvious euphemism for sex, possibly even reflecting her free indirect discourse—she wants him to lie with her, naked by her side, perhaps for hours.

The translation continues: "One day when he came into the house to see to his duties, and none of the household servants were there indoors, she caught him by his loincloth, saying, 'Come, make love to me,' but he left the loincloth in her hand and ran from the house." Why the Hebrew *beged*, "garment," has been transformed into a loincloth is something of a mystery—it could certainly have been a short Egyptian tunic, more likely for a chief steward, with no underwear. The general term, moreover, does a better job of carrying forward the motif of garments that runs through much of the Joseph story. Much worse, "make love to me" reappears instead of "Lie with me" in the original. The expression sounds more like what a yearning wife would address to her husband or lover than what an imperiously lascivious aristocratic lady would say to her young slave.

Let us continue with the lusting lady's words to the people of her household after Joseph has fled from her advances, leaving his garment in her grasping hand: "Look at this! My husband has brought in a Hebrew slave to bring insult on us. He came in here to rape me, but I gave a loud scream. When he heard me scream and call for help, he ran out, leaving his loincloth behind." The blunders of the Revised English Bible go on till the end of this episode, but what I have quoted up to this point should suffice to illustrate the general problem with the modern English versions of the Bible: because the translators do not see the artistry of the simple language of the original, they feel at liberty to rearrange it in ways that undermine it and to substitute wrong English terms for beautifully right ones in the Hebrew. In the sentences just cited, there are unfortunate choices at every step of the way. The Hebrew does not say "my husband" but merely "he." The point of this usage should have been obvious: in her effort to enlist the indignation of the household staff against both Joseph and her husband, Potiphar's wife does not refer to Potiphar by name, role, or title but only, angrily, as "he." The introduction of "husband," evidently motivated by the fear that readers might be incapable of figuring out who "he" was, blunts the biting effect of her dialogue. The next problem is "to bring insult on us." Apart from the fact that it is a little dubious as an English idiom, it entirely obscures the shrewd ambiguity of the Hebrew verb *tsaḥeq*, which does occasionally mean "to mock" but has an underlying sense of "to laugh," "to play," "to toy with," and "to dally with" (sexually)—for this last meaning, see Genesis 26:8, where it is used for Isaac disporting himself with Rebekah. This verb, then, archly invoked by Potiphar's wife, simultaneously suggests sexual dalliance and mockery, which might be conveyed in English by "toy with us" or "play with us." The next misstep in the translation is much worse. Having previously twice represented "to lie with" as "to make love to," the translation now lunges in the opposite direction and renders the same phrase as "to rape me." This lamentable choice of course entirely eliminates the link between her urging Joseph, "Lie with me," and what she now reports to the household slaves. It is an embarrassing instance of the misguided assumption of modern translators of the Bible that one must always render terms according to context, ignoring the lexical value of the Hebrew words. She is obviously claiming that Joseph attempted to rape her, but the Hebrew writer takes care to put in her mouth not a verb for rape, which she might have felt to be indelicate, but rather the very phrase she addressed in the imperative to Joseph. The most shocking distortion of this translation is that it has Potiphar's wife refer to Joseph as "the Hebrew slave." What the biblical writer takes care to have her say is "the Hebrew man" because she is addressing people who are themselves in all likelihood slaves, and so she doesn't want to mention a condition they share with Joseph but rather to enlist their solidarity as fellow-Egyptians who could be subject to the sexual depredation of this Hebrew man from the wild Semitic north. It is only when she repeats the very same speech to her husband that she strategically switches from "man," 'ish, to "slave," 'eved, because she wants to drive home the point to Potiphar that a vile slave, someone he owns, has presumed to assault her. The translators thus have obliterated the brilliant effect of a change within verbatim repetition in the dialogue.

In the final sentence of her false accusation of Joseph, there is no "call for help" in the Hebrew. The addition of that phrase reflects another misapprehension that compromises modern translations of the Bible. The translators appear to work on the assumption that readers of the Bible are rather dim and thus repeatedly need to have things spelled out for them. In the present instance, the translators evidently don't trust readers to realize that a woman's screaming from her bedchamber is a cry for help, and so they add the explanatory phrase. Finally, this version has Joseph flee, "leaving his loincloth behind," whereas the Hebrew reads, "he left his garment by me." The divergence may seem small, but it is unfortunate. The switch she has made in her lie is from the narrator's twice-stated report that the garment was left "in her hand" to its being left "by me." Her manifest implication is that Joseph removed his garment himself as prelude to assaulting her. The use of a general adverb, "behind" obscures the close spatial connection between her and the garment, and does not encourage us to visualize what the writer wants us to visualize—that the garment held tight in her hand is now misrepresented by her as lying alongside her. All this clearly shows that a great narrative depends not just on the details of the plot, which here are only somewhat distorted at a couple of points but not altogether altered, but on the particular words through which the story is told.

This transmogrification of the story of Joseph and Potiphar's wife is an object lesson in how translators of the Bible have stumbled because they have failed to see its literary shaping or to respect the subtlety and the accuracy of its word choices. There is a kind of literary art that achieves the most sophisticated effects through a seeming simplicity of language. This is true of some of the poetry of Emily Dickinson and Robert Frost and of almost all of Hemingway's prose. Let me cite just one example, from Hemingway's *The Sun Also Rises* (the lines occur in the first paragraph of chapter 4). There is no syntactic complication; the vocabulary is deliberately limited; and yet the evocation of a nocturnal cab ride in Paris shared by Jake and Brett is finely evocative: "We were sitting apart and we jolted close together going down the old street. Brett's hat was off. Her head was back. I saw her face in the lights from the open shops, then it was dark, then I saw her face clearly as we came out on the Avenue des Gobleins. . . . Brett's face was white and the long line of her neck showed in the bright light of the flares. The street was dark again and I kissed her." The diction of biblical narrative, which of course strongly influenced Hemingway through the King James Version, is a pre-eminent instance of complexity realized through ostensible simplicity. The King James translators, largely through their assumption of the inspired authority of Scripture in its literal formulations, established a splendid precedent in this regard, despite occasional lapses. They understood, at least intuitively, that a limited lexicon could work better than an expansive one, that repetition of terms could be a resource, that plain language could be better than highfalutin diction, and that the words of the Bible should be conveyed, not explained. It is a pity that their successors have learned so little from what they finely accomplished.

CHAPTER FOUR

Sound Play and Word Play

SOUND PLAY AND WORD PLAY are ubiquitous in literature, and they are an abounding presence in the Hebrew Bible, both in the poetry and in the prose. The limit case of such play with language is the pun, which is often essential to the meaning and just as often an insuperable challenge to the translator. Let me offer an illustration from English poetry that will be transparent to anyone who knows the language. John Donne, one of the great poets of the seventeenth century, who early in his career wrote some of the most splendidly sensual love poems in the English tradition, became an Anglican divine and an intensely religious poet, composing, among other spiritual texts, several penitential poems as he apprehended that his end was near. One of these, "A Hymn to God the Father" (despite the title, it is really a confession) comprises three rhyming stanzas, the first two of which conclude with the following lines, "When Thou hast done, Thou hast not done, / For, I have more." The repeated "done" clearly puns on his own last name. Any conceivable translator, unless willing to contort or distort the lines in order to somehow approximate the pun, would have to give it up, but much of the urgent point would be given up as well: God may seem to have done, but He must listen to another two stanzas of confession, so He neither has done nor yet has Donne. The concluding stanza enjoins God to pledge that at the moment of the poet's death His son—another pun referring both to "sun" and Christ—will shine, "And, having done that, Thou hast done, / I fear no more." Serious puns of this order of meaningful brilliance are the translator's despair, and there are many of them in the Bible.

Sound play and word play at least sometimes lend themselves to viable English equivalents, but puns rarely do. The translator may be able to find a partial, perhaps slightly awkward solution, though in many instances he or she may have to give it up, as the example from "A Hymn to God the Father" may suggest. It should be said that, with very rare exceptions, translators of the Bible have not even tried to work out solutions to this challenge. The same translators, after all, who ride roughshod over the Hebrew syntax and are obtuse about the word choices of the Hebrew writers would scarcely think that the play of sound of the Hebrew words or the way they inscribe double meanings was part of the translator's task.

Here are just a few instances of puns in which there is nothing much a translator can do. In 1 Samuel 25, when Abigail rushes out to head off David's band of men bent on vengeance against her obnoxious husband, she begins her shrewd speech to David with the following words, "Mine, my lord, is the blame!" (verse 24). But the first monosyllabic word in the Hebrew, *bi*, has a double meaning because its homonym has the sense of "please," or, more strongly, "I beseech you." Thus, the first syllable she utters sounds like the beginning of a plea, and would have sounded that way to David's ears, and only as the brief sentence unfolds do we realize that it has to mean "mine" (more literally, "in me"). This ambiguity jibes nicely with the content of her speech, which in fact is a kind of plea, but more substantively, a canny argument that David not shed her husband's blood but leave matters to God (or does she perhaps hint, to her?). It is hard to see how a translation can do anything with this play of homonyms: a nuance is lost, though rather less than would be lost in the translation of the Donne poem.

Some biblical puns are thematically important. Others are deployed as formal framing devices. The Hebrew writers often used the repetition of a word with a different meaning to mark the transition from one segment of a narrative or poem to another. When Ehud assassinates the Moabite king Eglon in Judges 3, he "thrusts" (*wayitqaʿ*) his sword into his victim's fat belly (verse 21). Then, having fled, as the next stage of his story begins, he "blasts" (*wayitqaʿ*) the ram's horn to rally fighters around him. The repetition of the verb in a different sense serves as a kind of bridge between successive episodes in the same narrative. The only way to convey this in English would be through some clumsy circumlocution such as "he let out a piercing sound with the ram's horn" after using "pierce" instead of "thrust" in the report of the assassination, but it is painfully evident that far more would have been lost than gained by this sort of wordy maneuver. Nothing of thematic importance is omitted by surrendering the pun, only the visibility of an elegant formal device. The same device is employed in the vivid poem that is chapter 7 of Proverbs. First, in the introductory verses in which the mentor exhorts the young man to heed his instruction before beginning his monitory tale, he asks him to "keep . . . my teaching like the apple of your eye [*'ishon*]" (verse 2), and then, as he launches his story of the seductress lurking for her prey as evening falls, he evokes that dangerous moment as "pitch-black [*'ishon*] night and darkness" (verse 9). There are other ways of referring to deep darkness in biblical Hebrew, but the poet chooses to use the homonym for the word that means "apple of the eye" in order to underline the formal link between the frame of the story and the story proper. This move cannot be conveyed in translation, but all that is lost is the perception of a formal design.

Occasionally, there are puns that are readily translatable. One that I have already mentioned in connection with word choices is the deployment of "hand," *yad*, in the story of Joseph and Potiphar's wife. As in English, to leave things in someone's hands (English usage calls for a plural) is to leave them in that person's trust, which Potiphar is repeatedly said to have done with Joseph. A translation should stick with the hand and not substitute an abstraction, for at the climactic moment of the story, "hand" no longer means "trust" but, as we have seen, is literally a hand—the grasping hand of Potiphar's wife in which Joseph leaves his garment as he flees her advances.

As I have noted, most of the biblical puns resist this sort of easy transference to English. But as anyone who has attempted to translate a great work of literature can attest, all translations are no more than approximations of the original, and in the case of puns, at least sometimes there are ways of approximating the double semantic effect of the Hebrew, even without an actual pun. Such efforts, I must confess, can be a bit awkward, but it seems to me better to try for equivalences than to give readers the misleading impression that the Hebrew has a single flat meaning. I will offer three small examples from the Book of Job, the work of the supreme virtuoso of biblical poets, whose lines, not surprisingly, are rich with puns and word play. In 7:6, as Job invokes the fleetingness of his life as grounds for God's ceasing to torment him he says, "My days are swifter than the weaver's shuttle. / They snap off without any *tiqwah*." It is worth noting the propensity of the Job poet to extend his metaphorical reach to realms unvisited by other biblical poets—industry, construction, horticulture, engineering, cheese-making, and more. *Tiqwah* is the common Hebrew word for "hope" so surely the half line needs to be rendered as "They snap off without any hope." But this same word has a homonym that means "thread," and thus the climax of the line is a pun that refers simultaneously to hopelessness and to the breaking of a thread on the weaver's loom. Obviously, there is no English equivalent for this double meaning. I have tried to intimate something of its effect by using "snap off" as the verb. Let me hasten to say that translation often involves painful compromise—you gain something through the loss of something else. The Hebrew verb here has the literal sense of "come to an end," which of course more clearly points to the idea of the hopeless end of life, but it seemed to me worth surrendering that nuance in order to convey to the reader the continuation of the weaving imagery in the second half of the line.

In 21:20, as Job wishes that God, referred to here with the archaic-poetic designation "Shaddai," would actually punish the wicked, he says, "let him drink from Shaddai's seething venom." Now the word I have represented as "venom," *ḥeimah*, also means "wrath," and it is etymologically linked to burning heat. Because the verb used is "drink," it seems likely that "venom" is the leading edge of the double meaning. If, as I have said, translation often involves compromise, it also sometimes necessitates a bit of perhaps forgivable cheating. There is no "seething" in the Hebrew, but "wrath" is readily associated with seething and seething with heat, so the introduction of a word not in the text may be justified as a way of suggesting the double edge of the Hebrew pun.

In 25:5, Bildad, one of Job's three adversarial comforters, in arguing that no one can be innocent in God's stern searching gaze, says, hyperbolically, "Why the moon itself does not give light, / and the stars are not clear in His sight." The pun here is in the verb attached to "stars." The Hebrew *zakhu* manifestly shows the root *z-k-h*, commonly used to indicate a state of legal innocence. But after the shining of the moon in the first verset, the poet is patently activating another word *zakh*, an adjective that means "bright" or "pure." Here it is pressed to serve as a kind of ad hoc verb, making the stars lack both innocence and light. In this case, "clear" in the translation replicates something of the double meaning of the Hebrew, though it is a weaker pun. That is, "clear" in English does have a legal sense, like the Hebrew (as in "cleared of all charges"), and in this context it also may suggest the immaculate light of the stars, though it lacks the connotation of brightness.

Occasionally, careful philological scrutiny is needed in order to see that what might be taken as a repetition is actually a pun. Here is the conclusion of God's curse upon the serpent in the King James Version: "I will put enmity between thee and the woman, and between thy seed and her seed; it shall bruise thy head, and thou shalt bruise his heel" (Genesis 3:15). The same Hebrew verb is used twice, but the translation just quoted introduces a double confusion because serpents bite rather than bruise and they certainly do not have heels. Modern translators generally repeat the verb in both clauses but substitute a different English equivalent, "strike," an imprecise representation of the Hebrew. The verb used in the original, *shuf,* means "to rub" and, by extension, "to trample" or perhaps even "to pulverize." But when the serpent is its subject, it means instead onomatopoeically "to hiss" (probably related to *sha'af,* "to pant") and through metonymy, "to bite," which is what poisonous snakes do. I gesture toward the pun by translating "He will bite your head / and you will boot him with the heel." This, of course, is less than a full pun, and perhaps "boot" as a verb is slightly awkward, but it seemed to me worth doing in order to convey something of the play of double meanings in the Hebrew.

As is apparent from the examples we have considered, conveying Hebrew puns in English is usually a highly imperfect undertaking, and in many cases it is altogether unfeasible. Sound play and word play offer the translator more latitude, although, as with puns, they are a feature of the Hebrew that has been almost entirely ignored in the existing English versions. The Bible begins with a piece of sound play that has, as I shall try to explain, some significance. Before God's creation of the world, a condition of primordial chaos prevailed, represented in the King James Version as "the earth was without form and void." Several modern versions adopt this language, merely modifying it slightly (e.g., "formless and void"). This formulation is a perfectly accurate representation of the meaning of the Hebrew, but what it leaves out is what happens in the sound of the Hebrew, which is *tohu wavohu*. (Interestingly, the Hebrew entered French as *tohu-bohu*, with the sense of "confusion.") Now, *tohu* is a well-attested word meaning "emptiness" or "void," and in one poetic text (Deuteronomy 32:10) it is associated with the trackless waste of the wilderness. *Bohu*, on the other hand, is unusual, and though one cannot be certain, it looks as if it might be a nonce word invented by the Priestly writer to rhyme with *tohu*. The effect would be similar to such English combinations as "helter-skelter" and "harum-scarum." My guess is that the writer wanted to strike a phrase in which the second term phonetically mirrored the first, suggesting how in the moment before the ordering acts of creation, everything was intermingled, everything spilled into everything else (and there is a similar suggestion in the two English analogues just cited, which indicate, respectively, breakneck haste and disorderliness or confusion). In translating the phrase, I could not think of an English pair of phonetically echoing words that accurately conveyed the meaning of the

Hebrew, and so I substituted alliteration for rhyme in the word pair, using "welter and waste."

The Hebrew writers, of course, themselves often used alliteration to significant effect. Psalm 30 is a thanksgiving psalm, evidently expressing gratitude for recovery from a near-fatal illness. Its concluding lines acclaim God for having transformed the condition of the speaker from desperate misery to joy. The first half of the penultimate line (verse 12) sounds like this in Hebrew: *hafakhta mispedi lemahol li*. A literal rendering would be: "You have turned my mourning into a dance for me." But the two Hebrew nouns, *misped* and *mahol*, alliterate, and this phonetic link is meaningful—God in His graciousness has taken a sad state, indicated by a word beginning with the Hebrew letter *mem*, and transformed it into its antithesis, indicated by another word beginning with the letter *mem*. In the process of translating, every once in a while you get lucky. As I pondered the effect of these two Hebrew antonyms beginning with the same consonant, it suddenly occurred to me that there was a perfectly good English word for a chant or lament intoned in mourning, such a lament being the precise meaning of the biblical *misped*, and that was "dirge," so the English line became "You turned my dirge to a dance for me," happily replicating the significant alliteration of the Hebrew and also, through the string of monosyllabic words, retaining the poetic rhythm of the line.

Among biblical poets, Isaiah is the great master of highlighting antithesis by juxtaposing words that sound alike but are opposite in meaning. He does this rather often because he wants to dramatize linguistically how things are the opposite of what they should be in the kingdom of Judah. Here is a line from one of his denunciations: "Your nobles are knaves / and companions of thieves" (1:23). In the Hebrew, the first of these two versets comprises just two words, *sarayikh sorerim*. The first of these two nouns can mean "noble," "officer," or "commander," so "noble" is a legitimate English equivalent. The second noun is literally "wayward ones," and thus "knaves" is not much of a stretch. Isaiah's alliteration is more complete than mine because it incorporates both the repetition of the initial *s* sound and a repetition of the consonant that follows it, *r*, which is actually doubled in the second word. The point of the sound play should be clear: the *sarim*, the nobles or commanders who ought to be setting a model for the people and leading them along paths of righteousness, have turned into *sorerim*, knaves, rebels, people turning off from the true way. Without some intimation in English of Isaiah's sound play, the force of this line of prophetic poetry is altogether lost.

The most common form of alliteration in the Hebrew is the use of paired words, usually but not invariably the same part of speech, either two nouns or two adjectives, that begin with the same consonant. The effect of the phonetic link is to bracket the two terms together as an interlocked unit or a doubled epithet. One such pair, which recurs several times, always attached to God, is *hod wehadar* (see, for example, Psalms 96:6), which I suggest rendering as "greatness and grandeur," though other solutions are possible. The existing English versions ignore the alliteration, which does, after all, introduce a rhetorical flourish, though working out an English equivalent is not very difficult. The first half of the Hebrew line in Job 15:24 begins with an alliterative pair of nouns, *tsar umetsukah*, literally, "foe and distress." I translate this as "failing and foe," reversing the order of the two nouns for the sake of the rhythm of the line. "Failing," of course, slightly modifies the meaning of "distress," but not, I think, unreasonably, and the alliterative flourish is worth preserving to convey the poetic strength of the line. In 19:27, toward the end of one of Job's expressions of his anguish, he moves from the outward flaying of his skin (verse 26) to the pain within him, in a line that would sound quite grotesque if rendered literally: "my kidneys come to an end in my lap." The Hebrew of this verset is *kalu kilyotay beḥeiqi*. "My lap" here obviously means "within me," and in biblical physiology the kidneys are imagined to be the organ of conscience, and so they are associated with sentient awareness. My nonliteral version, which does not really misrepresent the Hebrew, is "my heart is harried within me."

Let me offer one last example of alliteration from Job and how it might be conveyed in translation. One of many memorable moments in the great poem that is the Voice from the Whirlwind is the depiction of the warhorse snorting fiercely and galloping headlong across the battlefield. One verset in this spectacular description (39:24) sounds like this in the Hebrew: *beraʿash werogez yegamʾe-ʾerets* (in the first two words here, the accent falls on the second syllable where the repeated sound occurs, thus underscoring the alliteration). I translate the verset as "In clatter and clamor he swallows the ground." A more literal rendering of the second of the two bracketed nouns would be "rage" or "disturbance" (the verbal stem is used, for example, for the tossing of waves in the sea and for earthquakes). Translation inevitably involves a series of tricky judgment calls. Some may conclude that it is inadmissible to push "disturbance" as far as "clamor" but I think the Hebrew *rogez* itself exhibits a range of overlapping meanings and that the palpable power of the alliteration in the line is important to preserve in English.

We have already noted how Isaiah uses alliteration to highlight the contradiction between antonyms. Here is one more example (1:13): *lo' 'ukhal 'awen wa'atsarah*, which I translate "I cannot bear crime and convocation." Elsewhere, Isaiah often follows the more common biblical pattern of bracketing together related terms. Here is a train of three nouns that not only alliterate but also rhyme (22:5): *ki yom mehumah ume-vusah umevukhah*, which I approximate as "For it is a day of turmoil and trampling and tumult." This hews closely to the meaning of the three Hebrew nouns, though the last would more literally be "confusion." Isaiah's internal rhyming disappears in the English, but a translator can scarcely expect to equal the virtuosity of a great poet. I will cite one last example from Isaiah among many possible ones, in which, denouncing the priests and prophets who have betrayed their calling by plunging into drunken orgies, he castigates them for having *paqu peliliyah*, in my version, "juddered in judgment" (28:7). The Hebrew verb does mean "to quake" or "to shake" (it is especially used for the knees giving way), and I would concede that "juddered" for the sake of the sound, is a slightly odd word to introduce. The general issue is what kind of words are acceptable usage in a translation of the Bible. A word of this sort would be entirely inadmissible in the prose narratives because of the firm commitment in the prose, as we have seen, to limit the vocabulary. The Hebrew of biblical poetry, on the other hand, often incorporates unusual—even arcane—terms, which is precisely why the ancient scribes struggled with it and committed frequent errors in transmission. In this instance, Isaiah may in fact have chosen to make a bold new application of a term more commonly associated with shaky knees, perhaps to suggest a carryover to the realm of judgment of the drunken unsteadiness of the judges.

Occasionally in biblical poetry, one encounters an entire verset of alliteration that creates a spectacular effect: the second verset of Psalm 37:20 evokes the evanescence of the wicked through the following sequence of sounds: *kiyqar karim kalu be'ashan kalu*, literally, "like the meadows' green [others, "splendor"] they end, in smoke they end." I propose emulating the fine phonetic effect of the Hebrew as "like the meadows' green gone—in smoke gone." Still more remarkable, because alliteration and internal rhyme not only please the ear but create a kind of onomatopoeia, is this half line, Song of Songs 4:11: *nofet titofna siftey khalah*. A partial English equivalent, not to be found in any of the modern versions nor in the King James translation, is "Nectar your lips drip, bride." My version, as I have said, is only a partial equivalent of the Hebrew: it has one internal rhyme, like the Hebrew (NOfet titOF), and an internal alliteration of r-sounds in nec**t**ar, **d**rip, **b**ride, but it does not match the musical lushness of the Hebrew with its triple alliteration (n, f, t). The orchestrated sound conveys a sense of one thing flowing into another, in perfect keeping with the sensual fluidity of the erotic subject evoked. This striking chain of intermingling words must have been popular in the ancient period because it appears verbatim in another poem (Proverbs 5:3) where it is attached not to a beloved woman but to a dangerous seductress. Some of the other deployments of expressive sound that we have considered may have escaped the translators because they are unaccustomed to look for literary patterns in the Hebrew, but their failure to respond to the lovely musicality of this verset is a little perplexing because it is so arrestingly evident to anyone who reads the Hebrew. My suspicion is that such moments have been dismissed by the scholarly translators even when they may notice them because they regard them as no more than embellishments unimportant for understanding the meaning. My own contention is that meaning in the Bible or in any literary text cannot be reduced to lexical values, that it involves the communication of affect and can never be separated from the nuanced connotation of words and their dynamic interaction as they are joined through sound, through syntax, and through poetic or narrative context.

My final category of pointed play with language in the Hebrew text is word play. Many of the biblical writers are virtuosos of word play, and this is especially striking in the Prophets, so I will take all my examples from them. It is often possible, I think, to find approximate English equivalents for the playing of word with, or against, word, but of course this is not always feasible. Here are two lines of double word play from Zephaniah (2:4) that altogether resist transference to English. The literal sense of the line is "For Gaza shall be abandoned / and Ashkelon a desolation. // Ashdod at noon shall be banished / and Ekron be uprooted." The dire fate of these Philistine cities is clear enough in the English, but what is not visible is how this prophecy is reinforced by a kind of fusion of words. The Hebrew for "Gaza shall be abandoned" is *'azah 'azuvah* and for "Ekron be uprooted" is *'eqron te'aqer*. The effect is to intimate an indissoluble link between the name of each of the Philistine cities and the verb indicating destruction that immediately follows it, as though the doom of the city were somehow inscribed in its name. It is hard to imagine how this could possibly be conveyed in English.

In many other instances, however, a reasonably acceptable English equivalent can be found if the translator makes the effort, which manifestly has not been the case in the existing versions. Let me illustrate what might be done by citing one of Isaiah's deftest flips of a word to its like-sounding opposite. In the Song of the Vineyard (chapter 5), in representing Israel's ruining the precious vineyard given to it by God, he says (verse 7, which I shall first render literally) "And he hoped for justice [*mishpat*], and, look, a blight [*mispah*], / for righteousness [*tsedaqah*], and, look, a scream [*tse'aqah*]." Without any suggestion of the Hebrew word play in the English, the general semantic content of the line can be made clear enough, but its poetic-prophetic bite is altogether blunted. Isaiah makes his point by showing how a positive value, *mishpat*, is distorted into something that may sound alike but is the exact opposite, *mispaḥ*, and, in exactly the same way, how *tsedaqah* turns into an occasion for horror, *tseʻaqah*. With the importance of the word play in mind, I propose translating as follows: "And he hoped for justice, and, look, jaundice, / for righteousness, and, look, wretchedness." I duly note that this rendering of the line diverges somewhat from my general commitment to a relatively literal translation of the Bible, but I think the divergence is both limited and justified. "Jaundice" is a particular kind of blight and so really doesn't misrepresent the Hebrew. "Wretchedness" is a bit more of a stretch from "scream," though a person might well cry out in a condition of misery. What is essential, in any case, for conveying the sharpness of the Hebrew is to work out some English counterpart for the distorted echoing of sound in each of the pairs of words and how that very distortion expresses the perversion of justice that is the subject of Isaiah's castigation.

What is more common in the Hebrew texts, often in the poetry but also sometimes in the prose as well, is the pairing of two words exhibiting a link of meaning that is reinforced by the similarity of sound. We have already noted a couple of examples in connection with the use of alliteration. Here is a line of prophetic poetry that appears both in Isaiah 13:6 and Joel 1:5: "For near is the day of the LORD, / and like *shod* from *Shaddai* it shall come." Now, as we saw earlier, Shaddai is an archaic designation for the deity, its use by and large restricted to poetry. Because of its strong coloration as an old epithet for God, I have chosen here and elsewhere not to translate it but to preserve it as a name (the King James Version usually renders it as "the Almighty," but it is far from clear that this particular attribute of God is conveyed by the name). The Hebrew noun that precedes it, *shod*, suggests a violent act and is associated with a verbal stem that means "to loot, to despoil." What we can confidently assume about the meaning of the term is that it indi-

cates sudden disaster. The fact that it shares both of its consonants with "Shaddai" is significant: it is as if there were some
intrinsic, necessary connection between Shaddai and the cataclysm He is about to inflict on the day of the LORD. My own
attempt to intimate this in English is "a shattering from Shaddai." I was encouraged to make this choice because elsewhere
shod is alliteratively bracketed with the noun *shever*, which
does mean, quite literally, "shattering." But many choices in
translation end up being only partially satisfactory solutions,
and I must confess that this seems to me to be the case here. I
am a little unhappy with having used a three-syllable gerund
for a monosyllabic noun in the Hebrew. I thought about "a
shock from Shaddai" but concluded that "shock" was too much
restricted to emotional disturbance to serve as a general term
for disaster. I also considered, for a fleeting moment, "a shot
from Shaddai" but immediately realized that this was far too
colloquially modern. In the end, then, I settled on "shattering."
I share this weighing of alternatives with the reader in order to
make it clear that this is what translation is all about: you see
an important effect in the original; you balance different possibilities for conveying it in translation; sometimes you feel
you've gotten it just right; sometimes you adopt a solution that
is far from perfect but that is nevertheless preferable to not
communicating the effect of the original at all.

Here is a phrase from Ezekiel (33:28) where the imperfec-
tion of the solution may be more trivial. In a prose prophecy
about the impending doom of the kingdom of Judah, Ezekiel
represents God saying, "I will make the land a *shemamah* and
meshimah." The first of these two nouns, which has considerable currency in prophetic literature, means "desolation." The
second noun is a more unusual formation from the same verbal
stem that means more or less the same thing. The semantic
force of joining the two in word play is: "absolute desolation."

This is easy enough to reproduce in English as "desolation and devastation," though other variations are possible. The only reservation I have about my own solution is the use of two polysyllabic Latinate words. The words used in biblical Hebrew are for the most part quite compact, and as a general rule it is preferable to employ short English words in translation, which usually are Anglo-Saxon rather than Latin or Greek in origin. In some instances, however, the general rule has to be surrendered.

Here is a double word play from Isaiah 24:17, so striking that Jeremiah (48:43) appears to have borrowed it verbatim. The literal sense of the line is: "Fear and pit and trap / upon you, dweller in the land." The Hebrew of the first verset is *paḥad wafaḥat wafaḥ*. (I should explain that the initial *p* here and the two *f*'s that follow actually transliterate the same Hebrew letter *peh*, which, at least according to the Masoretic punctuation, becomes an *f* when preceded by a vowel. The alliteration is thus more visually evident in the Hebrew, and it is possible that the sounds of *p* and *f* may have been closer to each other in the ancient pronunciation.) The point of the repetition of sound is fairly obvious: the three similar-sounding nouns evoke a tight chain of disaster, and the next line conjures up an image of the person fleeing in fear unable to escape: "And he who flees from the sound of fear / shall fall into the pit, // and who comes up from the pit / shall be caught in the trap." I was tempted to translate the initial chain of nouns as "terror and tripwire and trap," but the Hebrew resisted this phonetic luxury because the middle term, *paḥat*, is clearly something one falls into and so has to be a pit. The necessary compromise, then, is: "Terror and pitfall and trap," which conveys the rhythm and some of the fusion of sound of the Hebrew without betraying the meaning of any of the three words.

In this overview of puns, sound play, and word play in the Hebrew text, I have meant to show that there are sometimes ways to get these effects across in English and sometimes not, with many in-between instances in which the translation succeeds only in part, or succeeds at a certain cost. If as a translator I am happy with some of my solutions, I have tried to be candid about others that seem to me in one way or another imperfect. But in reviewing these different manifestations of the verbal virtuosity of the Hebrew writers, I have sought to make clear that, as with other aspects of biblical style, this play with the sound of words is not ornamentation but, on the contrary, is intrinsic to the meanings of both the poetry and the narratives. Obviously, no representation of the Bible in another language can replicate the experience of the poems and stories available to an attentive reader of the original. Nevertheless, a conscientious translator should strive to fashion as many English approximations as may be feasible of the purposeful artistry through sound of the Hebrew. The alternative is a flattening of the biblical texts grounded in a misconception that their meaning is readily conveyed through the lexical values of the words used. The biblical lexicon is surely important, and translations ought to try to represent it faithfully and precisely, but the meanings of these writings—sometimes a flourish of emphasis, sometimes a pointed revelation—also flow from the sound of the words and the subtle ways in which they are linked with each other. Sound, of course, is not limited to phonetic kinship but is also manifested in rhythm, and we shall now go on to consider that aspect of biblical literature and what might be done about it in translation.

CHAPTER FIVE

Rhythm

LET ME BEGIN with the importance of rhythm in the narrative prose of the Bible because most of the English versions have made it quite inaudible to their readers. Having been enchanted by the Hebrew of the Bible since late adolescence, I thought that over the years I had identified the principal stylistic virtues that made the language of these ancient stories so captivating and such a subtle instrument for conveying moral vision, character, theme, and narrative circumstance. When, however, I began the task of translation, I was immediately compelled to realize that there was one aspect of biblical prose style that I had omitted from my unwritten checklist, and that was rhythm. I was barely halfway through the first chapter of Genesis when, without at first knowing why, I rendered the report of the creation of the celestial luminaries as follows: "And God made the two great lights, the great light for dominion of day and the small light for dominion of night, and the stars" (Genesis 1:16). After committing these words to paper, I paused to ask myself: Why did I opt for "dominion"? There is a grammatical reason for this choice, but it was secondary for me. That is, although almost all the English versions use an infinitive (as we saw in the first chapter, "to rule," "to govern," "to dominate"), the Hebrew actually uses not an infinitive but a verbal noun derived from the root that means "to rule." Hewing as much as feasible to the literal contours of the Hebrew, I had reached for a noun instead of an infinitive in English. But then it dawned on me that my choice was more decisively determined by another consideration: listening to the sound of my English version of this sentence, I discovered that I had produced a rather close approximation of the Hebrew cadence. The original for the second part of the verse sounds something like this (uppercase letters mark the syllable where the accent falls): *'et-hama'OR hagaDOL lememSHElet haYOM we'et hama 'OR haqaTON lememSHElet haLAYlah we'et hakokhaVIM.* The priestly writer who composed this verse is, when he is at his narrative best, the stateliest of biblical prose-masters. His version of creation proceeds through a series of beautifully choreographed cadences that are a stylistic concretization of his vision of orderly harmony in the creation of the world. An English representation of his account of God's making the sun and the moon and the stars that failed to emulate the cadence of the verse also would fail to convey adequately the sense of cosmic harmony it expresses. "Dominion," in each instance followed by an unstressed syllable and then a stressed syllable, as in the Hebrew, decisively confirmed the cadence, and I realized that I had unconsciously chosen it because its pattern of stresses was identical with *memSHElet.* From this point onward I was keenly aware of how important it was to reproduce in translation some approximate equivalent of the Hebrew prose rhythms, to the extent that this was feasible within the limits of English.

The only complete English version of the Bible that in part accomplishes this is the King James Version. (The translations of the Five Books of Moses and the Former Prophets by Everett

Fox, following the model of the Buber-Rosenzweig German version, also have rhythm very much in mind, although he does not always hear the same rhythms I do.) The 1611 translation exhibits a good deal of rhythmic integrity—though it is far from consistent—in part because it follows the syntactic configurations of the Hebrew and in part because the seventeenth-century translators, unlike their modern successors, had a good ear for literary English. The translations of our own era have been for the most part arhythmic, and the occasional satisfying cadence would seem to be virtually accidental because the translators show little awareness that cadences are a vital dimension of the Hebrew prose. Indeed, it is hard to imagine any artful prose (at least in the languages I can read) that is not rhythmic in significant ways. Rhythm is the beating heart of literary prose, and as in the relation of the heart to the human body, arhythmia can be life-threatening to the writing.

Let me propose an analogy for what has happened in modern English versions of the Bible. Let us suppose that the manuscript of *Moby-Dick* falls into the hands of a zealous copyeditor. He thinks it's a pretty good story but that he can improve it, perhaps make its language a bit more dignified. Where Melville says, scarily, that the whale "has no face," our dutiful editor substitutes "countenance." Where Melville's narrator pays tribute to the drowned cabin-boy Pip with these words (the very last words of chapter 27), "called a coward here, hailed a hero there," the resolute reviser changes this to "stigmatized as a coward here, celebrated as a hero there." This would manifestly be a case of a conventionally decorous and unimaginative editor disastrously getting in the way of a bold and original writer, which is by and large what has happened with modern English renderings of the language of the Bible. After our interventionist editor was finished with *Moby-Dick*, one would still be able to recognize the outlines of a strange and interesting tale about a monomaniacal one-legged sea captain in pursuit of a great white whale, but the magic of Melville's great novel—its mesmerizing iambic cadences reminiscent of Shakespeare and Milton, its powerful alliterative constellations, its echoes in rhythm as well as in diction of the King James Bible—would be gone. That is more or less the general effect of modern translations of the Bible. A reader will certainly be able to see what is going on in the stories—though, as we have observed in our consideration of word choice, he or she will be led to miss many of the subtleties or the pungency of what is going on—but the significant shaping music of the prose will have vanished.

A translator's successes, which inevitably occur in the midst of half successes and partial failures, are occasionally quite visible to readers, as, for example, when he gets lucky and manages to find a happy English equivalent for a pun in the original. Successes of rhythm, however, are likely to be invisible to most readers, and they will be chiefly gratifying to the translator himself, though I think that at least subliminally they contribute in some way to the satisfying experience of the narrative for the reader. A case in point is the Parable of the Poor Man's Ewe that the prophet Nathan declaims to David (2 Samuel 12). Nathan, having gotten word of David's adulterous liaison with Bathsheba and his murder of her husband Uriah, comes to David and presents him with the parable. It functions very much like the play-within-the-play in *Hamlet* ("The play's the thing / wherein I'll catch the conscience of the king"). That is, the parable is a veiled representation of the king's crime, and when David, not seeing this, expresses outrage at the act of the rich man in the parable, Nathan points an accusatory finger at him: "You are the man." (Shakespeare in fact may have had the story of David and Bathsheba in mind because there is another detail in *Hamlet* that looks like a connection with 2 Samuel 11: Rosencrantz and Guildenstern are sent off with a sealed document that is their own death sentence, just as Uriah is in the biblical story.)

What is scarcely evident in the English versions is that the language of the parable, and most emphatically its rhythms, set it off from the surrounding narrative. It is also set off lexically from the larger narrative, but this distinctiveness can scarcely be intimated in translation. In the three and a half verses of this brief text, there are three nouns that are not used in the framing story (two of them never and the third just once)—the terms for "poor man," "wayfarer," and "traveler." Elsewhere the word for "poor man," *r'ash*, occurs primarily in Wisdom texts, mainly in Proverbs, and thus predominantly in poetry; *heilekh*, "wayfarer," appears only here; *'oreah*, "traveler," shows only three other occurrences in the biblical corpus. The very vocabulary of the parable thus would have signaled to the ancient audience that this is a different kind of story from what precedes and follows, but, unfortunately, there is no satisfactory way of getting this across in English, though of the three English equivalents I have proposed for the Hebrew terms, "wayfarer," as a slightly archaic noun, might perhaps offer a hint of what is suggested in the original. More to our present purpose, the rhythm of the parable clearly differentiates it from the surrounding narrative. It does not scan as poetry, but it does exhibit a pronounced regularity, at several points a kind of singsong pattern. Here is a transliteration of the first sentence, short pauses marked with a single forward slash and a longer pause with a double forward slash: *shney 'anaSHIM haYU / be'IR 'ahAT // 'ahAD 'aSHIR / we'ehAD RA'SH.* My English version, an attempt to sing along with the singsong of the Hebrew, reads: "Two men there were in a single town, one was rich and the other poor." (There is a certain generic kinship with the opening words of the frame story in Job, "A man there was in the land of Uz—Job, his name," though because this is a parable no names are admissible.) The rhythmic evocation of the loving care that the poor man lavishes on his little ewe is especially notable: "From his crust she would eat and from his cup she would drink and in his lap she would lie, and she was to him like a daughter." The Hebrew here is: *mipiTO to'KHAL / umikoSO tishTEH / uveḥeiQO tishKAV / wateHI-lo keVAT.* Each of the four nouns here is monosyllabic, though the first three have a possessive suffix added ("his"). As a translator, I was very happy when I realized that I could reproduce the first three emphatic monosyllabic words, *pat, kos, ḥeiq,* as "crust," "cup," and "lap," though the concluding monosyllabic noun *bat* had to be given up for the less rhythmically satisfactory "daughter." Needless to say, the existing English versions, including even the King James Version, offer scarcely a suggestion of this rhythmic pattern in the Hebrew.

But why, the skeptical reader may well ask, is it at all important? Minimally, one could say that there is something aesthetically satisfying in the way the compact rhythmic regularity of the parable sets out its narrative details. Yet I think there is more involved in the deployment of a distinctive rhythm in the parable. What it would have communicated to the early listeners to the story, whose vernacular was Hebrew, would have been a strong sense that this was neither a historical narrative, like the David story, or the report of an actual case, as David first takes it to be, but rather a tale told in the never-never land of parables where people are not assigned names and there is a schematic opposition between rich man and poor man, householder and wayfarer. The point of all these signals of genre is precisely that David doesn't get it. He construes a palpable parable as the account of an actual chain of events, vehemently condemning the rich man and thus setting himself up for Nathan's withering declaration that he is the very man figured in the parable. The episode of David and Bathsheba is in

more ways than one the great turning point in the whole David
story. In the early part of the narrative, David showed himself
to be canny and politically astute, this attribute serving as a
chief resource in his rise to power. But with his sexual appro-
priation of another man's wife and his bungled effort to cover
up his act by contriving the husband's death, he begins to lose
his astuteness. Indeed, the scheme of getting rid of a rival by
having him killed on the battlefield exactly replicates Saul's
clumsy plan to have David killed at the hand of the Philistines.
When David, then, fails to see what the audience would have
immediately known, that the parable is a parable, he is exposed
as a once-savvy political actor whose grip has become shaky.
The rhythm that distinguishes Nathan's words from the larger
narrative as a parable is far from being merely decorative: it
tells us through a pattern of sound that the king who has lost
his way morally is missing something essential at this moment.
The general point is that rhythm in literary narrative is not only
pleasing but in many cases meaningful, as Melville's Shake-
spearian iambic cadences convey to the reader a sense that his
novel is not just an odd tale about the crazed captain of a whaler
but high tragedy, a story with cosmic reach.

Such highly explicit deployment of rhythm as in Nathan's
parable is obviously not typical, but rhythm serves a variety of
purposes across a spectrum of prose narrative in the Bible from
the grand epic cadences of the Flood story to the rhetorical
emphases of the speeches in Deuteronomy with their lengthy,
rhythmically balanced periodic sentences, a stylistic feature
that rarely occurs elsewhere in the Bible. It may be instructive
to consider an example in which rhythm is a little less salient
but nevertheless significant.

The beginning of the Book of Exodus reflects an important
shift in the nature of the narrative after Genesis. The Patriar-
chal Tales had brought us close up to the tensions and intrigues

and struggles of familial life in homey settings, with a probing focus on individual character. Exodus switches to a wide focus as the biological "sons of Israel" (which is to say, of Jacob) become, as the King James Version words it, "the children of Israel" (which is to say, Israelites), members of a "people," a term first attached to them in Exodus 1:9. As Pharaoh turns hostile to the Israelites in his country, a cycle of repression and resistance through persistent propagation manifests itself, and something of the movement of this cycle is inscribed in the rhythm of the prose. Here is my version of Exodus 1:8–14, which I do not claim to be perfect but which represents an effort to provide some English equivalent for the Hebrew cadences (forward slashes indicate what I perceive as the boundaries between small rhythmic units):

> And a new king arose over Egypt / who knew not Joseph. / And he said to his people, "Look, the people of the sons of Israel / is more numerous and vaster than we. / Come, let us be shrewd with them lest they multiply / and, then, should war occur, / they will actually join our enemies / and fight against us and go up from the land." / And they set over them forced-labor foremen / so as to abuse them with their burdens, / and they built store-cities for Pharaoh, / Pithom and Rameses. / And as they abused them, so did they multiply / and so did they spread, / and they came to loathe the Israelites. / And the Egyptians put the Israelites to work with crushing labor, / and they made their lives bitter with hard work / with mortar and bricks and every work in the field—/ all their crushing work that they performed.

Readers are not likely to pay conscious attention to the rhythmic aspect of these verses in translation but the passage does, I think, have a degree of rhythmic integrity, in part realized by the preference given to compact English words and the avoidance of polysyllabic Latinate terms (with the signal exception of "multiply," chosen because of its echo of "be fruitful and multiply" in the Creation story) and in part by the adherence to the Hebrew parataxis. The last eight syllables of my version are an iambic sequence that is slightly different from the Hebrew but imparts a sense of rhythmic closure as does the Hebrew. There is a sweep of epic panorama in the narrative report that is registered in the balanced cadences in such sentences as "And as they abused them, so did they multiply and so did they spread, and they came to loathe the Israelites." My version is by no means put forth here as an impressive achievement, but it does strive for fidelity to the measured cadences of the Hebrew that reinforce the large historical scope of the story.

The English renderings of the modern committees, though they convey the same narrative data, make it sound like a different kind of story. Here is the Jerusalem Bible's version of these seven verses:

Then there came to power a new king who never heard of Joseph. "Look," he said to his people, "the Israelites are now more numerous and stronger than we are. We must take precautions to stop them from increasing any further, or if war should break out, they might join the ranks of our enemies. They might take arms against us and then escape from the country." Accordingly they put taskmasters over the Israelites to wear them down by forced labor. In this way they built the store-cities of Pithom and Rameses for Pharoah. But the harder their lives were made, the more they increased and spread, until people came to fear the Israelites. So the Egyptians gave them no mercy in their demands, making their lives miserable with hard labor: with digging clay, making bricks, doing various kinds of field-work—all sorts of labor that they imposed upon them without mercy.

This modernizing translation is probably the most egregious of all the twentieth-century versions, but the others are not much better. I will not comment on all the lamentable diction because that is an issue we took up in the previous chapter. The forward movement of the prose is interrupted by the tic of explanatory phrases—"accordingly," "in this way," and, most shamefully, an entire clause that has no equivalent whatever in the Hebrew, "So the Egyptians gave them no mercy in their demands." The impulse to spell out everything for the reader at the cost of both rhythm and stylistic decorum is especially evident in "We must take precautions to stop them from increasing any further." The Catholic translators are not alone in this kind of misguided maneuver. Their Protestant counterparts in the New English Bible render this clause as "We must take steps to ensure that they increase no further." If you try to read out loud either of these versions of this clause, it will be immediately evident that there is no detectable rhythm at all. These are words that, both in sound and diction, could easily come from a bureaucratic report or a pedestrian newspaper article. And the destruction of rhythm is reinforced throughout the passage by the jettisoning of parataxis. The cadenced grandeur of the Hebrew writer's narrative of the oppression of the people of Israel in Egypt can scarcely be heard in these English versions.

In regard to poetry, the modern English versions do make various efforts to convey some sort of rhythmic regularity because the translators are obviously aware that rhythm is an important property of poetry, even if they evidently do not realize that this is also the case for prose. What they fail to represent in translation is that rhythm is a consistent, defining feature of poetry that cannot be maintained for a line or two and then recklessly discarded. As in other aspects, the King James Version manages things better than its successors do, but, as we had occasion to observe of its treatment of Job 3:11, it can slip from a rhythmically tight verset to a completely slack one. Let me begin with a concise illustration, two lines from Psalm 30 (verse 9). The 1611 translators render these as follows: "What profit *is there* in my blood, when I go down to the pit? Shall the dust praise thee? shall it declare thy truth?" I will now set alongside this three modern versions. The Jerusalem Bible: "What point is there in my death, my going down to the abyss? / Can the dust praise you or proclaim your faithfulness?" The Revised English Bible: "What profit is there in my death, / in my going down to the pit? / Can the dust praise you? / Can it proclaim your truth?" The Jewish Publication Society: "What is to be gained from my death, / from my descent into the Pit? / Can dust praise You? / Can it declare Your faithfulness?"

It should be observed that the King James Version handles quite aptly what in the Hebrew is the second line of poetry, marking a strong rhythmic pattern: "Shall the dust praise thee? shall it declare thy truth?" (The Hebrew sounds like this: *hayodKHA 'aFAR hayaGID 'amiTEkha.*) The three modern versions, by hewing fairly closely to the King James translation, also do fairly well with the rhythm of this line, though two of them damage the final cadence by substituting the trisyllabic "faithfulness" for the compact "truth." The 1611 rendering of the first of these two lines is less successful rhythmically. What creates a patch of arhythmia in the initial verset is the insertion of the two words "is there," italicized because they are not in the Hebrew and seem to have been inserted for the sake of clarity. But a literal representation of the Hebrew at this point is perfectly intelligible in English: "What profit in my blood?" This stripped-down version has the virtue of almost literally reproducing the cadence of the Hebrew: *mah BEtsa' b^edaMI.* Apart from the issue of rhythm, one might note that all three modern versions substitute "death" for the strikingly concrete "blood" in the Hebrew, evidently not trusting readers to realize that "blood" means "death," in keeping with the general assumption that metaphor and metonymy are unintelligible to modern readers. It is also apparent that the modern tendency to explanatory paraphrase has the effect of converting the sound of poetry into the amble of expository prose: "What point is there in my death, my going down to the abyss" and "What is to be gained from my death, from my descent into the Pit?" The loss of rhythm is compounded by a perhaps inescapable loss of sound play. The first three words of the initial Hebrew verset, transliterated above, have a pounding insistence through the strong alliteration of m's and b's. I could not see how to do this in English but reached for compensation by generating an alliteration in the second verset. My translation of the whole line reads as follows: "What profit in my blood, / in my going down deathward?"

This example highlights a general challenge in rendering the rhythms of the Hebrew poems in English, which is their terrific compactness. A larger issue of the transposing of poetry from one language to another is involved. Every poetic tradition quite naturally exploits and actually builds on the distinctive properties of the language that its poets use. Classical Greek, for example, distinguishes between short and long vowels, and the verse composed in the language, designated "quantitative," works through a regular sequence of short and long syllables. The meter of the Homeric epics is dactylic hexameter. Various experiments have been made to create an English equivalent, but because our language does not make this distinction between short and long vowels, quantitative verse in English is not really viable, and even attempts to render Homer in dactylic hexameters based on stress rather than quantity have not been notably successful, probably because the English ear does not readily adapt itself to a line of this length. Some adjustment for the requirements of the target language are obviously necessary. At the opposite extreme, literate Englishmen in the age of Alexander Pope tended to assume that narrative poetry worthy of the name had to be cast in rhyming iambic pentameter couplets, and that is how Pope translated Homer. Now Pope was one of the great technical virtuosos of English poetry, and in some respects his Homer is a tour de force. The heroic couplets (as they are technically called), however, combined with the employment of eighteenth-century English poetic diction, are quite distant from the sound and feel of Homer's archaic poetic world, and Pope, as has often been observed, ends up making the Achaean warriors of the Iliad sound a bit too much like English gentlemen. At the opposite pole from Pope, Richmond Lattimore's 1951 translation of the Iliad may be regarded as a turning point in the English rendering of ancient poetry. Its general thrust was to suggest in English something of the archaic concreteness and directness of Homer's language and its sound and to avoid making it resemble the poetry of the age in which the translation was composed. Lattimore's Homer has been criticized for a certain ungainliness of formulation and for its metrical flaws. Though it was quite influential in its time, a whole spate of competing translations have ensued over the years, of which perhaps the most successful is the somewhat free version by Robert Fagles, who did both Homeric epics. Nevertheless, Lattimore established a precedent that I think is still valuable in considering what to do about biblical poetry.

It is of course impossible to create a very close equivalent in English of the sound of biblical poetry. The most basic problem is the phonetic and morphological concision of biblical Hebrew. It contains relatively few polysyllabic words. This is an issue that may be addressed by favoring short English words, usually of Anglo-Saxon rather than Latin or Greek origin; that is a strategy that is often feasible but not always. The more challenging aspect of brevity in biblical Hebrew is the synthetic character of the language: pronouns are usually not stated for verbs but simply indicated by how the verbs are conjugated; pronominal objects of verbs are merely marked by suffixes attached to the verbs; possessive pronouns of nouns are also indicated by suffixes, and there are no compound tenses of verbs; the present tense of the verb "to be," moreover, is merely implied. Thus, the five words of "the LORD is my shepherd" represent just two in the Hebrew, *Yahweh ro'i*, and there is no way of getting across this particular compactness in English. Rhythmically, most lines of biblical poetry comprise two halves or versets (some also show three members rather than two); and, most commonly, each verset has three accented syllables, though there is a range from two to four, and the number of unaccented syllables between the stresses is not fixed. All this makes the sound of ancient Hebrew poetry quite different from that of modern English poetry. What should be avoided is transforming the rhythms (and diction) of biblical verse into something that sounds altogether like indigenous English poetry, modern or otherwise. In this respect, the precedent of Lattimore's Homer is useful: a translator should be executing repeated *gestures* toward the sound and feel of the ancient poem, even if the nature of the language of translation works against any complete replication of them. A certain tamping down of English is required, cutting back the proliferation of syllables and eliminating unnecessary words (as in our example from Psalm 30, "What profit *is there* in my blood?" where eliminating the two italicized words rescues the rhythm). Isaiah 1:4 illustrates this general issue concisely. The Hebrew of the first line of poetry in this verse sounds like this: *HOY GOY ḥoTEI'/ 'AM KEved 'aWON*. As the uppercase syllables indicate, there are three beats in each verset, and there are also three words in each verset, with a total of nine syllables in the line. As the transliteration shows, the line begins with an emphatic internal rhyme in two successive stressed syllables, and I see no way to reproduce that in English. The King James Version renders the line as "Ah, sinful nation, a people laden with iniquity," and several modern translations follow it closely or even entirely. "Ah, sinful nation" is aptly cadenced and diverges rhythmically from the Hebrew only by the unstressed syllable at the end. But "a people laden with iniquity" is arhythmic, the culprit being the Latinate polysyllabic "iniquity," a choice probably influenced by the Vulgate that should be strenuously avoided by translators. The one modern translation that does something effective with this line is the New Jerusalem Bible: "Disaster, sinful nation, / people weighed down with guilt." "Disaster" is a somewhat odd choice for the Hebrew *hoy* (an interjection that I render as "woe"), and I suspect that, at least subliminally, it may have been dictated by an impulse to produce an iambic sequence, and I would not quarrel with that. Iambs are the most natural rhythmic pattern in English, and though there is rarely an equivalent in the Hebrew, the evocation of iambic cadences makes the rendering of the Hebrew sound like proper English poetry, although obviously the metrical regularity of strict iambic lines must be avoided. My own proposal for rendering this line in English reads as follows: "Woe, offending nation, / people weighed down with crime."

Here is a line of poetry (Job 3:3) where my own translation adopted iambs for one verset precisely with the aim in mind of intimating some connection with a prevailing pattern of English poetry: "Annul the day that I was born, / and the night that said, 'A man is conceived.'" The initial verb here caused me some distress. The King James Version and most of its modern successors use "perish," which is a good lexical equivalent of the Hebrew but in modern English might sound a bit prissy (because it now survives in phrases such as "perish the thought"). A couple of modern translators, seeking to give punch to the line, show "damn the day," which is a strong sound but introduces a notion of either damnation or slightly vulgar speech in no way implied in the Hebrew. To return to the issue of rhythm, after the introduction of a verset that scans as iambic tetrameter, the second verset in my translation is looser rhythmically, as the Hebrew very often is, resembling the original in showing four stressed syllables, like the first verset. Here is a transliteration of the line in Hebrew: *YO'vad YOM 'IWAled BO / wehaLAYlah 'aMAR HOrah GAver.* There is a neat alliteration in the first two words of the Hebrew line that had to be given up. Otherwise, the first verset shows a regular pattern of stressed syllable / unstressed syllable / stressed syllable, for which my iambs are an English equivalent, and the second verset, loosening the pattern, introduces more unaccented syllables between the stresses in the first three words. "A man is conceived" is not as good rhythmically as would be "A man's conceived," but, after some struggle, I concluded that contractions were a bit too informal for the stylistic decorum of biblical poetry. There are, of course, other ways that this line might be translated effectively, but I hope my version shows how something of the distinctive rhythmic force of the Hebrew may be conveyed in English while working with the intrinsic metrical momentum of English verse.

While modern English versions of the Bible, as we have seen, pay almost no attention to the aspect of rhythm in the narrative prose, the treatment of poetry is mixed, with rhythmically satisfying lines intermingling with ones that sprawl and stumble. Much the same can be said of the representation of poetry in the King James Version. My guess is that the intermittent moments of apt rhythm by the moderns derive from an awareness on the part of the translators that poetry, after all, should have a certain harmony or regularity in the way it sounds. The problem is that the translators do not keep this in mind consistently as an important aspect of the rendering of poetry, and they repeatedly let go of it as they concentrate on what they conceive to be lexical fidelity to the Hebrew (although the fidelity, as I argued earlier, very often proves to be questionable), and consequently for many stretches of the poems the translators do not appear to have listened to the sound of their own words.

Let me illustrate the oscillating character of the treatment of poetry by lining up four versions of the opening passage of Psalm 45, beginning with the King James Bible. This psalm is a celebration of the heroic stature of the king on the occasion of his marriage to a foreign princess. The first part of the poem extols the king's virtues; the second part, which I will not quote, is explicitly an epithalamion, evoking the pomp and circumstance of the royal wedding. The 1611 translation begins as follows: "My heart is indicting a good matter: I speak of the things which I have made touching the King: my tongue is the pen of a ready writer." With all due respect to the collective genius of the committees convened by James I, one has to say that this is scarcely recognizable as poetry: it corresponds to one triadic line in the Hebrew in which each of the three versets has four words and four accents, but it represents the line with twenty-eight English words and no perceptible rhythm. In the next lines, the translation finds its way to something like the music of poetry: "Thou art fairer than the children of men: grace is poured into thy lips: therefore God hath blessed thee forever. Gird thy sword upon thy thigh, O most mighty, with thy glory and thy majesty." But this happy moment is immediately followed by a backslide into arhythmia: "And in thy majesty ride prosperously because of truth and meekness and righteousness; and thy right hand shall teach thee terrible things."

The New Jerusalem Bible is a modern version that, for once, actually manages better than the 1611 translation: "My heart is stirred by a noble theme, / I address my poem to the king, / my tongue the pen of an expert scribe." The English rhythm fashioned for this triadic line is admirably apt, and it does what I have proposed a translation should do with the sound of the original—evoking it while remaining faithful to the intrinsic metrical logic of English verse. The next verset maintains this rhythmic integrity, "Of all men you are the most handsome," but then the rhythm begins to slip: "gracefulness is a dew upon your lips, / for God has blessed you for ever. / Warrior, strap your sword at your side, / in your majesty and splendour advance, ride on / in the cause of truth, gentleness and uprightness." What is particularly noticeable here is how polysyllabic terms for abstract qualities—"gracefulness," "gentleness," "uprightness"—break the rhythm and make the lines hard to read as poetry.

The skidding in and out of rhythm is markedly audible in the Revised English Bible's handling of these lines. It begins promisingly with a verset almost identical to the one in the Catholic translation: "My heart is astir with a noble theme." Then, however, it stumbles into limp prose: "in honour of the king I recite the song I composed, / and my tongue runs swiftly like the pen of an expert scribe." The translators then regain their metric balance with "You surpass all others in beauty; / gracious words flow from your lips, / for you are blessed by God for ever. // Gird on your sword at your side, you warrior king, / advance in your pomp and splendour, // ride on in the cause of truth and justice. / Your right hand will perform awesome deeds." All this works quite nicely, though even here, characteristically, one verset, "ride on in the cause of truth and justice" loses grip on the rhythm. It should be noted that a good deal of the rhythm-spoiling in this version is the result of that impulse to clarify and explain which we consider in relation to word choice: "in honor of," "I recite the song I have composed," "in the cause of," all terms of which the Hebrew is quite innocent.

Finally, the Jewish Publication Society version begins as follows: "My heart is astir with gracious words; / I speak my poem to a king; / my tongue is the pen of an expert scribe." So far the translators have maintained fairly simple diction, and that correlates with a degree of rhythmic integrity. They continue in this manner for the next two versets: "You are fairer than all men; / your speech is endowed with grace." But then the third verset of this triadic line loses rhythm altogether: "rightly has God given you an eternal blessing." The next lines read as follows: "Gird your sword upon your thigh, O hero / in your splendor and glory; // in your glory win success; / ride on the cause of truth and meekness and might; / and let your right hand lead you to awesome deeds." All of the translators appear to have struggled with these concluding lines, and it should be said that the final verb, of which "right hand" is the subject, could derive either from a root that means "to teach, to guide" or (my own preference) one that means "to shoot." The JPS translators, like their counterparts, seem baffled about what to do with these lines semantically, and the rhythm disappears as they flounder.

I will now offer my own attempt to represent these lines in readable English poetry that is reasonably faithful, rhythmically and also lexically, to the Hebrew. This is not intended as a triumphal gesture—I hasten to say that the more successful lines in the four cited versions are quite as good as my own. The difference in regard to rhythm is that I have done my best not to neglect it at any point, as the earlier versions egregiously do. The lexical aspect of my translation, though it is linked only obliquely to rhythm, requires a note of explanation. As with the prose, I have sought to represent the Hebrew literally unless that seemed altogether untenable. Thus, instead of the explanatory "matter" or "theme" at the beginning of the psalm, I use the plain term of the Hebrew, "word," assuming that the poet as proud craftsman celebrating the king wants to call attention to the basic unit of his medium. And instead of "noble" or "gracious" as the modifier, I have the primary word reflecting the Hebrew, "goodly" (it could also be simply "good"). At the end of this line, my version makes the scribe not "skilled" or "expert" but "rapid," which is what the Hebrew literally says. I would concede that this might be a miscalculation. What I wanted to do was to preserve the concreteness of the original: someone who can move his pen quickly over the parchment scroll is of course an expert scribe, and I thought, perhaps misguidedly, that readers would immediately realize this. More confidently, I am happy with "what I made," which is surely preferable to "the things which I have made" or "the song I composed." The Hebrew is a noun that literally means "my makings" or "my acts," and the poet's presentation of his poem as something made or fashioned seems to me preferable to substituting the referent of the making, "poem" or "song." Here is my version of these four lines:

> My heart is astir with a goodly word.
>> I speak what I made to the king.
>>> My tongue is the pen of a rapid scribe.
> You are loveliest of the sons of man,
>> grace flows from your lips.
>>> Therefore God blessed you forever.
> Gird your sword on your thigh, O warrior,
>> your glory and your grandeur.
> And in your grandeur pass onward,
>> mount truth's word and meek justice,
>>> and let your right hand shoot forth terrors.

A metrically strict English version of the metrically freer Hebrew is to be avoided, or it will slip into the problem of Pope's iambic pentameter Homer. Fidelity to the Hebrew in fact leads one at certain points to depart somewhat from rhythmic regularity, and this may be desirable. "You are loveliest of the sons of man" is a little loose rhythmically, though I don't think it abandons rhythm altogether as do quite a few lines in the examples cited above. It is then followed by the rhythmically tight "grace flows from your lips." One aspect of sound beyond rhythm here is the emphatic alliteration in the third line of *hodKHA wehadaREkha*, which I have represented as "your glory and your grandeur," whereas the other translators have ignored the alliteration.

This review of my English version of these lines should suggest my sense that all translations are imperfect things. As a translator, you find yourself constantly weighing sound against meaning, fidelity to the original against idiomatic aptness in the target language, and you are often not entirely sure that you have made the right decision. What needs to be kept in mind in regard to the considerations of this chapter is that both in biblical poetry and in prose the carefully crafted cadences are inseparable not only from the beauty of the writing but also from its nuanced meanings. The dimension of sound would have been all the more urgent for the first audiences to whom these texts were addressed, who would of course not have read them silently but rather would have listened to them. As I have tried to make clear through these various examples, it is not feasible or even desirable to produce an exact replication of the rhythmic patterns of the Hebrew, but some evocation in English of the strong rhythms of the Hebrew is indispensable in order to convey an adequate sense of what is compelling about biblical literature.

CHAPTER SIX

The Language of Dialogue

DIALOGUE IS THE VITAL CENTER of biblical narrative. Proportionally, at least in the great chain of narratives from Genesis to the end of 2 Kings, it takes up a large amount of space in relation to the narrator's reports. The contrast between the two is striking. Narrative report in the Bible often uses drastic summary. A journey of many weeks by Abraham's servant from Canaan to Mesopotamia is conveyed in a single verse, as is Jacob's long trek on foot along this same route. Even more extremely, nearly two decades in the life of Jacob and Esau are telescoped into a single Hebrew verb and noun, "And the lads grew up," and a similar contraction of narrative time occurs in the report of baby Moses growing to a man. In stark contrast, when something significant is happening in the story, it is generally represented through dialogue, where, of course, there is an equivalence between narrated time and narrating time.

For the biblical writers, then, it was clearly of paramount importance to show people relating to each other through speech. What is noteworthy is that the Bible provides a remarkable early precedent for novelistic dialogue. Erich Auerbach, in the celebrated first chapter of *Mimesis*, famously found in

biblical narrative rather than in Homer the foundational precursor for the novel's representation of what is portentous and
sometimes tragic in the familiar routines of daily life. The sup-
ple shaping of dialogue—not an issue with which Auerbach
deals—as a manifestation of individual character and social or
moral location is a correlative of this perception. Let me hasten
to say that there are, of course, many wonderful speeches in
both the Iliad and the Odyssey, but, by and large, they are
speeches, often running on for dozens or even hundreds of
lines, rather than the kind of interactive exchanges we associate
with novelistic dialogue. This may well be still another reflection of the difference between oral-formulaic composition in
verse and composition in prose through writing. The Homeric
bard, locked into a regular march of hexameters (in all likelihood, to the accompaniment of a stringed instrument), impro-
vising the details of his traditional story with the aid of set
verbal formulas, did not have the same flexibility as the prose
writer in altering the contours and even the diction of represented speech, though he could on occasion give his characters
great eloquence.

I noted earlier that biblical dialogue, though it does not appear to be directly mimetic of Hebrew speech, incorporates
significant gestures toward the vernacular. Because its linguistic register is not altogether that of the surrounding narrative
prose, it constitutes an early instance of the phenomenon of
"heteroglossia" that M. M. Bakhtin identifies with the novel—
that is, the joining or confrontation in a single text of different
modes of speech or sociolects within what is ostensibly the
same language. Perhaps the most memorable biblical instance,
registered in part but not entirely by several of the English versions, is the first words spoken by Esau in his story—and it is
worth noting again that in biblical narrative a personage's first
words are generally a strategic exposition of character. Esau,

famished after an unsuccessful hunt, says to his brother, literally, "Let me gulp down [or even more rudely, "cram my maw
with"] that red-red" (Genesis 25:30). The King James Version,
choosing not to admit anything so indecorous in Scripture, entirely fudges this: "Feed me . . . with that same red pottage." At
least two modern versions get the general idea, using "gulp" as
the verb and "red stuff" for what Esau wants, though the New
Jerusalem Bible follows the King James Version in translating
blandly "that red pottage." I don't think "red-red" by itself works
in English, so the addition of "stuff" seems a reasonable solution. None of the English versions except mine reflects the repetition of "red" in the Hebrew. It is a small but instructive point.
The impatient, hungry Esau cannot manage to come up with
the ordinary Hebrew word for "pottage," and instead he gestures toward the simmering pot, sounding like a toddler or
someone who barely knows the language, as he refers to its
contents as "this red-red." The repetition of the adjective, which
also highlights an etymological pun on the name of the people
he will father, perfectly expresses Esau at this point in his story
as the embodiment of inarticulate appetite, and as such it
should be reproduced in translation ("this red-red stuff").

As to the verb used here, an explanatory note will show what
it tells us about the general deployment of language in biblical
dialogue. The Hebrew verb *hil'it* occurs only here in the entire
biblical corpus. In rabbinic Hebrew, it is used for the feeding,
perhaps even forced feeding, of animals, and though we cannot
be sure it had precisely this meaning almost a millennium before the rabbinic texts, it seems probable that it indicated a
ruder kind of eating than the usual Hebrew verb. The writer in
this instance has violated a tacit rule of biblical narrative, di-
verging from its set use of primary terms only. My inference is
that the writer could not resist the temptation to put in the
mouth of Esau a crude eating word, elsewhere excluded from

biblical narrative, in order to underscore the initial characterization of the firstborn twin as a brutish figure. (Much later in
the story, he will seem to have changed rather surprisingly.)
What is instructive in this linguistic detail is what it reveals
about the willingness of the biblical writers to bend language
in dialogue in order to represent the distinctive nature of character or of the specific situation of the character. Let me now
proceed to a more complex example in which there is more
work for the translator to perform in order to convey the liveliness of the Hebrew dialogue.

We had occasion earlier to observe the use in Genesis 20 of
'elohim in the plural denoting "the gods," a sense missed by all
the English versions. Abraham is a new monotheist diplomati-
cally addressing a polytheist, and he treats the Hebrew noun
as a plural, invoking its polytheistic sense. There is more, however, of interest in the dialogue between Abraham and the in-
dignant local king Abimelech. Abraham has come to Abimelech in Gerar impelled by famine and has passed off Sarah as
his sister, whereupon Abimelech takes her into his harem. God
then appears to Abimelech in a dream vision and tells him,
"You are a dead man because of the woman you took, as she is
another's wife." The initial phrase is just two words in the Hebrew, *hinkha meit*. Some translators word it conventionally as
"you shall die." At least two modern versions show "you are to
die," a choice that has a certain philological justification because the presentative (*hinkha*) followed by a participial form
of the verb does often indicate an action about to happen. What
is lost, however, is the expressive *abruptness* of the two Hebrew
words: God altogether startles Abimelech by suddenly appear-
ing to him in a dream and immediately announcing, before any
explanation is offered, that he is as good as dead. I thought of
rendering this in three English syllables as "you are dead," but
that has a finality not quite suggested by the Hebrew, and so I

settled on "you are a dead man," which, though it is five words for two, reproduces something of the stark quality of God's words in the original.

Abimelech's response to God then gives the language an odd, and instructive, twist: "My Lord, will you slay a nation even if innocent?" The various English versions normalize this as "will you slay innocent people" or some variant of that phrasing, but I think the Hebrew is deliberately strange and that the strangeness needs to be preserved in the translation. The Hebrew does not say "people" but, pointedly, "nation" (*goy*). Why is this language assigned to Abimelech? In this instance, the motive is not characterization but the signaling of an intertextual link. Abimelech is presumably talking about himself as the embodiment or representative of the nation he rules. But the slaying of an innocent nation harks back to the immediately preceding episode (Genesis 19), the destruction of Sodom and Gomorrah, about which Abraham had bargained with God (Genesis 18), pleading with Him not to destroy the cities of the plain if there should be ten innocent (the same word used here) men within them. One should not assume that Abimelech knows anything about the destruction of Sodom and Gomorrah, but through the somewhat deformed sentence that the writer puts in his mouth, we are invited to imagine that he might be venturing an oblique reprimand to the deity: Are You up to your old tricks again, destroying nations even when there are innocent people within them, as I am innocent of this accusation? The odd formulation in the Hebrew illustrates why translators should be cautious about regularizing what may be deliberately irregular in the original.

Abimelech continues his protestation of innocence: "Did not he say to me, 'She is my sister'? and she, she, too, said 'He is my brother.'" The Hebrew, which my version follows quite closely, expresses a splutter of indignation on the part of

Abimelech: not only did Abraham pass her off as his sister but the woman herself—"she, she" seconded him in the deception. The modern versions regularize this with a bland "she also said," thus bleaching the biblical dialogue of its vivid color. A general aspect of the innovative character of dialogue in the Bible is involved here. Reported speech in the Hebrew narratives is often shaped to express a range of emotions and attitudes from confusion and embarrassment to cunning calculation (as in Jacob's words to Esau in the selling of the birthright) to indignation, as in the present instance. I cannot think of a close equivalent in ancient literature to this strongly mimetic articulation of dialogue. The exchange between Abraham and Abimelech the morning after the king's unsettling dream vision provides another example of this phenomenon. Abimelech first berates Abraham for the act of deception ("Things that should not be done you have done to me"). Abraham does not immediately respond, and the set formula for introducing speech is repeated with a brief statement by Abimelech: "And Abimelech said to Abraham, 'What did you imagine when you did this thing?'" As elsewhere, when the formula for introducing speech is repeated with no intervening response reported on the part of the interlocutor, this repetition signals to the audience that the second party to the dialogue has a problem about answering (as a result of amazement, embarrassment, confusion, awkwardness, or sheer surprise). Abraham momentarily flounders, then tells Abimelech the truth, that he was afraid the locals might kill him in order to take possession of his wife; but not wanting to admit to an outright lie about Sarah's being his sister, he goes on to say, "And, in point of fact, she is my sister, my father's daughter, though not my mother's daughter, and she became my wife." Whether such unions were licit in the ancient Near Eastern world is uncertain. (Scholarly ink has been spilled on the question.) What may be a clue to how Abraham is positioning himself is the unusual locution he uses, *wegam-'omnah*, which I have translated as "And, in point of fact." It seems to me a reasonable educated guess that this is some sort of legalism, part of what looks like a verbal smoke screen that Abraham is putting up in order to defend the dubious claim he made upon his arrival that Sarah was his sister.

Here is a more extreme example than Abimelech's "she, she" of the purposeful bending of language in dialogue for a mimetic effect. When Ahimaaz races from the battlefield to report to David the victory over the forces of the usurper Absalom, the king, after hearing of the victory, anxiously inquires about the fate of his son, "Is it well with the lad Absalom?" (2 Samuel 18:29). Ahimaaz, who knows that Absalom has been killed against David's strict orders, responds with Hebrew words that are incoherent, both syntactically and semantically, and that then break off. I translate them as follows: "I saw a great crowd to send to the king's servant Joab, and your servant, and I know not what . . ." All the English versions, proceeding from the naïve assumption that anything anyone says in the Bible has to make sense, "correct" this into intelligible English. The JPS rendering is typical: "I saw a large crowd when Your Majesty's servant was sending your servant off, but I don't know what it was about." This entirely masks the patent confusion of the Hebrew. What is surely going on is that Ahimaaz, afraid to tell the king that his son has been killed, dissolves into incoherence, his response an awkward stammer that he is then unable to complete. David himself is impatient with this breakdown of communication, the bearer of tidings having proven to be useless, and so he peremptorily orders Ahimaaz, "Turn aside, stand by!" It is a small token of the mimetic range of biblical dialogue that when the occasion requires, it can represent the failure of speech. (Just one biblical scholar has clearly seen this— Gary A. Rendsburg, in a 1998 article, "Confused Language as

a Deliberate Literary Device in Biblical Hebrew Narrative.")
Regrettably, one could scarcely guess this from the existing English versions.

The expressive flexibility of biblical dialogue is often put to excellent use in an area of representation that is one of the distinctive achievements of biblical narrative—everyday domestic life with all its problems of conjugal strife, jealousy, sibling rivalry, and sometimes misdirected or frustrated desire. Here is the verbal interaction between God and Sarah in the annunciation of the birth of her long-promised but never-delivered son. God, whom Abraham had taken to be merely a human wayfarer, is addressing Abraham with Sarah eavesdropping on the conversation from just within the tent: "And he said, 'I will surely return to you at this very season and, look, a son shall Sarah your wife have'" (Genesis 18:10). All the English versions, beginning with Tyndale and the King James Bible, regularize the word order as "Sarah your wife shall have a son." But as we saw in the chapter on syntax, "fronting" is often an expressive device, and it is surely important that God's speech places that impossible, frequently desired thing, a son, at the very beginning of the clause. Although the next sentence (verse 11) is the narrator's report, not dialogue, it is worth a brief comment because the inadequacy of the translations here continues into the dialogue that follows. My version reads, "And Abraham and Sarah were old, advanced in years. Sarah no longer had her woman's flow." The King James Version handles this fairly aptly: "Now Abraham and Sarah were old and well stricken in years, and it ceased to be with Sarah after the manner of women." The literal sense of the last phrase in the Hebrew is "like the way of women," and so this is a nice English equivalent, but I thought that the indication of a postmenopausal condition perhaps should be a bit clearer and so opted for "woman's flow." The modern translators, for cultural reasons I would rather not contemplate, simply don't know what to do with language referring to bodily functions, especially those related to sexuality. Here is how they represent this sentence: "Sarah had ceased to have her monthly periods" (the New Jerusalem Bible)—"periods" is a modern term that manifestly violates the decorum of the ancient language, and why do we need "monthly" (were there annual ones?). The JPS version uses the same term to stumble into a different kind of awkwardness: "Sarah had stopped having the periods of women." (Had she switched then to having the periods of men?) The Revised English Bible, on the other hand, entirely gets rid of the discomfiting reference to menstruation: "Sarah being well past the age of childbearing."

These difficulties carry on into Sarah's dialogue—it is in fact an interior monologue but overheard by the omniscient divine guest—that immediately follows. The most egregious bowdlerizing is that of the Revised English Bible, still steering clear of the body and sex: "So she laughed to herself and said, 'At my time of life I am past bearing children, and my husband is old'" (verse 12). The New Jerusalem Bible lexically misses a crucial point in the Hebrew though it does pick up another, despite an unfortunate rearrangement of the Hebrew syntax. "Now that I am past the age of childbearing, and my husband is an old man, is pleasure to come my way again?" It is important to leave the clause about the husband's old age to the end because Sarah appears to tack it on, either as an afterthought, that not only she but her husband is aged, or as an oblique act of blaming— how would I have pleasure with such a decrepit husband? The JPS comes close to an adequate rendering: "Now that I am withered, shall I have enjoyment—with my husband so old?" The word translated as "withered" is a term used for the wearing out of garments through long use. I prefer "shriveled" to "withered" because it seems to me a bit stronger, but perhaps there is not much difference between the two. In any case, this word chosen for Sarah's interior speech powerfully conveys the plight of an old woman—she is said to be ninety!—once celebrated for her beauty who now sees herself as a dried-up bag of shriveled skin and bones. The terrible poignancy of her predicament as she expresses it to herself is entirely concealed in all the English versions except the JPS. I would prefer "pleasure" to "enjoyment," as did the 1611 translators, because the Hebrew shows a verbal stem strongly associated with sensuality and sexuality (it has the same triliteral root as "Eden"). My own rendering of this brief sentence of interior monologue, which seeks to preserve its potent sense of female physicality, is: "After being shriveled, shall I have pleasure, and my husband is old?" The strong embodiness of biblical narrative, especially in the dialogues, is spectacularly evident here: Sarah, a very old woman, bitterly contemplates her time-eroded body and thinks of the impossibility of what she hears promised by the speaker outside the tent: that she will not only experience the joy of becoming a mother but— what he did *not* say—achieve pleasure in the act of conception. Every term of her reported speech has been beautifully calculated to convey the physicality of her plight of childlessness in old age, and each of those terms needs to be honored in translation.

As we have seen, the modern versions often butcher an entire piece of dialogue, but what is more common is that they get a few things right and enough others wrong to compromise the general force of the dialogue. Joseph's exchange with his brothers during their first journey to Egypt (Genesis 42:7–18) is one of the most psychologically and thematically fraught dialogues in the Bible, and every term of the reported speech— even, as we shall see, verb tenses—serves to carry forth this weight of implication. The exchange between Joseph, the vice-regent of Egypt, and his brothers, who do not recognize him, begins simply enough: "And Joseph saw his brothers and recognized them, and he played the stranger to them and spoke harshly to them, and said to them, 'Where have you come from?' And they said, 'From the land of Canaan to buy food'" (my translation). Most of the English versions, reasonably enough, render this last phrase as I have. But because the verb used, *sh-b-r*, is not the ordinary word for buying, the JPS decides to represent the phrase as "to procure food." The verb in question, I should note, elsewhere means "to break." It is conceivable that its use here is dictated by the locution "to break [or stave off] famine," and that would equally apply to the noun for "food," *shever*, that also occurs in this story. But "procure" is patently a stylistic blunder: it is a verb at home in the directives of a quartermaster corps, or in an arrangement for prostitution, and not in an ancient Hebrew dialogue. Joseph proceeds to accuse his brothers: "You are spies! To see the land's nakedness you have come!" Here the JPS version, following the precedent of the King James Bible, preserves the language of nakedness, but other modern versions, again working from the assumption that all metaphors need to be explained, show "the country's weak parts," or even "the weak points in our defense," eliminating not only the sexual reference but even, in the last example, the land. Now the Hebrew noun Joseph uses, *'erwah*, means the sexual part of the body that must be covered—it is the term that occurs in the prohibitions of incest. The sense of the land—always feminine in the Hebrew—as a vulnerable female entity with secret parts that should not be exposed and of spying as a kind of violation is entirely lost by these curiously Victorian renderings. The brothers then seek to defend themselves with these words: "No, my lord, for your servants have come to buy food. We are all the sons of one man. We are honest. Your servants would never be spies." The tenses, or more properly, aspects, of biblical verbs are tricky to determine because they correspond at best only approximately to the tense system of English. Some of the modern versions represent the final verb here as a flat present tense, "are," but I think that is wrong because the Hebrew uses the perfective form, *hayinu*, of the verb "to be." The JPS, while persisting here in having the brothers "procure" food, is somewhat better with "we have never been spies." But it seems to me that the situational logic of this moment of dialogue does not call for a declaration of past activity but rather for an affirmation that this is not an activity they would ever engage in, and the form of the Hebrew verb allows that sense ("would never be"). In a moment, we will see a graver error in regard to verb tense.

Joseph's immediate rejoinder to his brothers is to repeat his accusation: "No! For the land's nakedness you have come to see." Their response is: "Twelve brothers your servants are, we are the sons of one man in the land of Canaan, and, look, the youngest is now with our father, and one is no more." None of the English versions, old or new, reproduces the syntactic fronting of "twelve brothers" although it is in fact thematically important to place those two words at the head of the sentence. The tense of the verb is a more critical issue. The Hebrew has no verb, only the predicate "twelve brothers" and the subject "your servants," which is how the present tense of "to be" is indicated. The King James Version gets this right, but almost all the modern translations "correct" this to "we were." The misguided motive is supposed logic: since these ten brothers know that one of the twelve "is no more"—he is certainly absent because they sold him into slavery and, they may assume, probably dead—the translators want them to say that they once were twelve but are no longer twelve. This change unfortunately erases the brilliant dramatic irony that runs through this whole dialogue. The brothers in fact *are* twelve, as Joseph knows perfectly well, and their use of the present tense when they say this to him makes them, in a pattern of dramatic irony, the conduit for information of which they are unaware, and which will be splendidly confirmed in the reuniting of all twelve brothers at the climax of the story. The final phrase of their response to Joseph, "and one is no more," triggers an outburst of anger in him, for it is a reminder of their brutal act in selling him as a slave, and so he says, "That's just what I told you, you are spies." The outburst is muted in all the English versions because they make it more formal, "It is as I have said," "As I have already said," and, only a little better, "It is just as I have told you." All such dilutions of the force of the Hebrew stem from the misconception that the speakers in biblical dialogue should express themselves in proper balanced sentences and that emotions or sudden spurts of feeling are not part of the articulation of language in the dialogues.

The draining of the vitality of biblical dialogue in English translations is manifested in two ways: a failure on the part of the translators to understand that language is being used expressively to reflect personality, narrative situation, social position, and much else, and an insensitivity to the nuances of language that would be appropriate for ancient speech (as in the "procuring" of food in Egypt). Let me cite two small examples of the latter problem in the reported speech we have been following in Genesis 42. When Joseph sends off the brothers, detaining Simeon as a hostage, he tells them, in my translation, to "bring back provisions to stave off the famine in your houses." The JPS, again floundering with that pesky word *shever*, renders this as "take home rations for your starving households," evidently unaware that rations are the kind of food you would find in an army mess-tin, not in the saddle-packs of camels in the ancient world. In the next sentence, moreover, of Joseph's final words to his brothers, both the JPS and the New Jerusalem Bible have him saying that they must come back with Benjamin so "that your words may be verified," unconscious that "verify" is something you do with documents or the results of an experiment, whereas the decorum of the Hebrew narrative requires a term such as "confirmed" (or in the King James Version, "proved").

Here is another instance in which the English versions get some things right but enough other things wrong to compromise the beautiful aptness of the Hebrew dialogue. In the Jephthah story (Judges 11), one recalls that the Israelite warrior makes a vow that if he returns victorious from the battle, he will sacrifice to God whatever or whoever first comes out of his house as he comes back, and, alas, this proves to be his only daughter. Here is the wrenching exchange between them in my English rendering:

> And it happened when he saw her, that he rent his garments, and he said, "Alas, my daughter, you have indeed laid me low and you have joined ranks with my troublers, for I myself have opened my mouth to the LORD, and I cannot turn back." And she said to him, "My father, you have opened your mouth to the LORD. Do to me as it came out from your mouth, after the LORD has wreaked vengeance for you from your enemies, from the Ammonites." And she said to her father, "Let this thing be done for me: let me be for two months, that I may go and weep on the mountains and keen for my maidenhood, I and my companions." And he said, "Go."

Let me immediately say that my version is more literal than any preceding one, including even the King James Version. Beyond my general conviction that it is wise to render the Hebrew fairly literally as far as English usage allows, there is a particular reason for the literalism here that will emerge as we consider the specific translation choices. At the beginning of Jephthah's speech, the King James Version also preserves the "laying low" ("thou hast brought me very low"), respecting the Hebrew verb, which is associated with forcing someone to

kneel or prostrate himself in defeat. At least two modern versions do away with the clear physical indication of the verb:
"Oh, my daughter, what misery you have brought upon me!"
(New Jerusalem Bible); "Oh, my daughter, you have broken my
heart with calamity" (Revised English Bible). The problem
with such interpretive and explanatory treatment of the Hebrew—"you have broken my heart" sounds like something from
a country-music lament—is that it obscures the notion the ancient writer had clearly in mind that Jephthah is using a military term: the warrior chieftain, victorious in battle, now dis-
covers that his own daughter, by coming out first from the
house to meet him, has devastatingly, if unwittingly, defeated
him. In my translation, Jephthah goes on to say, "I myself have
opened my mouth to the LORD." No other English version adds
"myself," but it conveys a nuance indicated in the original: in
biblical Hebrew, one does not ordinarily use a personal pronoun with a verb because the person of the verb's subject is
clearly marked by the conjugation of the verb. When the pronoun is added, as here (*'anokhi*), it is in order to place special
emphasis on the pronominal subject of the verb: "I myself,"
Jephthah confesses, have done this terrible thing, have pronounced this irrevocable vow. Something of the anguished father's psychology is intimated in this small turn of speech, and
it should not be invisible in translation.

The language of vow-taking is a still more crucial aspect of
this dialogue. The 1611 translation, like mine, represents it literally in both Jephthah's speech and his daughter's as "opened
my/your mouth." All the moderns clearly think this is too
strange (or perhaps even too obscure) in English, and so they
opt for "made a vow," "uttered a vow," or even, altogether in-
appropriately, "made a promise." There are two reasons why
the literal sense is important to preserve, though one of them
will be necessarily invisible in any translation. The idiom used

involves a thematic pun on Jephthah's name, which in fact means "he opens" or "he will open," thus prefiguring his ill-considered tragic vow. More to the purpose of viable translation, Jephthah's world is an archaic, virtually pre-monotheistic world in which a vow to a deity, as both father and daughter unquestioningly assume, is an irrevocable utterance that, once having issued from the mouth, has an irreversible efficacy and cannot be taken back. The language of translation should be appropriate for a story that took place long ago not only in regard to diction but also in regard to the ancient sense of reality, which I believe to be the case for these freighted words coming out of Jephthah's mouth. What, moreover, is the appropriate term for the irreversibility of the vow? At least two prominent modern translations have Jephthah say that he "cannot retract" his solemn vow. As one might expect from the modern versions, this is a mistake in diction—one retracts a statement made to the press, not a sacred vow. But it is wrong in another way because the verb Jephthah uses, "I cannot turn back," is crucial for the thematic configuration of the story. Since the 1920s, following the insight of Martin Buber and Franz Rosenzweig, students of the Bible have known, or certainly should have known, that biblical narratives are very often constructed through the repetition of thematic keywords, or *Leitwörter*, typically involving subtle plays on the different meanings of the same term. At the beginning of Jephthah's story, he is driven from his home into the badlands by his brothers, who evidently are abetted by the elders of Gilead. When the elders come to him in order to persuade him to lead the tribal forces against the Ammonites, they say, "Therefore now we have come back to you"—a slightly odd choice of verb (since they have not been there before) motivated by the overarching pattern of the keyword. Jephthah begins his response to them by saying, "If you bring me back" (the causative conjugation of the same verb). Jephthah is the banished brother who comes back first to his town and then victorious from the battle in what proves to be a disastrous return home. When he tells his daughter, then, "I myself have opened my mouth to the LORD, and I cannot turn back," using the reiterated verb in a different sense, his words are fraught with a painful irony. Needless to say, the irony is lost if the verb is translated as "retract" or even "renounce."

Let me offer one final brief example of how English translators simply have not paid attention to the fine modulations of biblical dialogue. When Ehud, concealing a short sword under his garment, bent on assassinating the Moabite king Eglon, enters the monarch's upper chamber, he says to the king, "A secret word I have for you, King" (Judges 3:19). Now the fronting of "A secret word," as in the Hebrew, is itself important because Ehud has placed it at the very beginning of his speech in order to get the king's attention and to motivate him to send all his attendants out of the room. This strategic turn of syntax is of course ignored in all the English versions, which choose to "normalize" the word order. But still more important in this bit of dialogue is how Ehud addresses the king. Ancient Near Eastern societies were manifestly hierarchical, and an elaborate decorum of language embodied this hierarchy. As we see abundantly in biblical dialogue, there were highly deferential formulas for addressing a monarch or a superior, and it was very often done in the third person, though Ehud, pointedly, uses the second person. The Israelite assassin discards this linguistic protocol for royalty, beginning his speech abruptly with the "A secret word" (a locution altogether drained of its power in the Revised English Bible's rendering, "I have a message for you in private") and holding back the title of his royal interlocutor, "King" until the very end of his sentence—a verbal maneuver that borders on rudeness, which Eglon chooses to ignore in his eagerness to hear the secret word. At least two English translations following the King James Version represent this as a formal address, "O King," though that is not necessarily indicated in the Hebrew, in which Ehud appears to throw in the title almost as an afterthought. Still worse, the Jewish Publication Society has Ehud say "Your Majesty" and the Revised English Bible introduces "my lord king," with both translations placing this dignified form of address at the beginning of Ehud's speech instead of at the end. The brutal abruptness of the way he turns to the king, as well as the king's inattention to a form of address that might be insulting rather than urgent, entirely disappears.

I want to reflect for a moment on this manhandling of the Hebrew because it is symptomatic of the broader failure to do justice to the dialogue in the English versions. Both these modern committees of translators make their misguided decision because they seek to have the reported speech conform to the propriety of conventional language rules. In conventional usage, you begin your address to the king by saying "Your Majesty" or "my lord king." (The translators are probably remembering the Shakespeare they read in high school.) Because you are the lowly subject and the king is your powerful superior, they assume that you are obliged to use some deferential epithet in addressing him. All this tilts the dialogue in a way the Hebrew does not suggest. It does not occur to the translators that in the Bible's innovative deployment of dialogue, linguistic norms may on occasion be deliberately violated for expressive effect. In this scene of an impending assassination, Ehud ignores court protocol in the way he frames his speech, luring the Moabite king with the prospect of a secret word that will prove to be a hidden sword thrust into the fat royal belly. These brief words are a vivid illustration of the fact that very often more is going on in biblical dialogue than one might assume.

What is true of dialogue is equally true of all the other aspects of biblical style that we have considered. Both the narrative and the poetry of the Bible deploy an extraordinary imaginative use of language that has very few equals in the whole ancient world and none among the geographical neighbors of ancient Israel. These formidable literary resources were of course usually marshaled for what we must call, lacking a better term, religious ends, but the full breadth of nuanced perspective on the interactions between the human and divine realms will not be visible in translation if the stylistic subtleties of the original are ignored. As I have repeatedly conceded in the course of this study, those subtleties do not always lend themselves to adequate representation in another language. The point, however, is that a translator needs first to see them and then to attempt to do something with them in translation, and the lamentable fact is that this has very rarely been the case. Even with the best intentions, any translation of a great work will sometimes prove to be a sorry thing. Translations, as I have conceded several times, are inevitably approximations of the original, but all of us engaged in the enterprise need to aspire to closer approximations. That is what I have sought to do in my own translation of the Bible. The great pity is that others, certainly among the modern versions, have failed to understand that the effort is necessary, and, indeed, indispensable. The Hebrew Bible gathers together a wide variety of literary texts that are quite often vivid, finely nuanced, and even sometimes startling in their stylistic articulations. A translation, for all the challenges it may confront, has the capacity to convey much of this liveliness and complexity if only the resources are summoned to do it.

SUGGESTED READINGS

Robert Alter, *The Art of Biblical Narrative*, Basic Books, revised edition, 2011. A general introduction to the conventions and techniques of biblical narrative that devotes some attention to word choice and repetition.

Robert Alter, *The Art of Biblical Poetry*, Basic Books, revised edition, 2011. A general introduction to the formal configurations of biblical poetry that tracks their modulations through different poetic genres.

Walter Benjamin, "The Task of the Translator," in *Illuminations*, edited by Hannah Arendt, translated by Harry Zohn, Harcourt, Brace & World, 1968. This essay has become a touchstone of theoretical speculation on translation. At points it is somewhat opaque, and it proceeds from a rather metaphysical conception of language.

David G. Burke, John F. Kutsko, and Norman W. Jones, editors, *The King James Bible at 400*, Society of Biblical Literature, 2013. A large collection of essays on the King James Version that looks both at its language and at the history of its subsequent impact.

Harry Friedman, *The Murderous History of Bible Translations*, Bloomsbury, 2016. A panoramic history of the translation of the Bible into many languages. Clearly a popularization, it abounds in vivid examples and lively anecdotes, though there are also simplifications and inaccuracies and no real sense of style in translation.

Hannibal Hamlin and Norman W. Jones, editors, *The King James Bible after 400 Years*, Cambridge University Press, 2010. A collection of essays that begins with two articles on the style of the King James Version and then focuses on its subsequent influence on many different writers.

Gerald Hammond, "English Translations of the Bible," in *The Literary Guide to the Bible*, edited by Robert Alter and Frank Kermode, Harvard University Press, 1987. An incisive account of English renderings of the Bible from Tyndale to the twentieth century that is alert to their problems and argues for the continuing superiority of the King James Version.

Robert Kawashima, *Biblical Narrative and the Death of the Rhapsode*, Indiana University Press, 2004. A compelling argument that biblical narrative's composition in writing enabled aspects in which it was a precursor to the novel. This analysis makes clear why word choice and narrative point of view are essential to maintain in translation.

Stanley E. Porter and Richard S. Hess, *Translating the Bible: Problems and Prospects*, Sheffield Academic Press, 1999. A volume of essays that begins with four that seek to frame the issues in regard to translation theory. An article by Richard S. Hess instructively illustrates questions of philology in translating the first five chapters of Judges, though only glancing attention is given to literary style.

Werner Schwarz, *Principles and Problems of Biblical Translation*, Cambridge University Press, 1955. A scrupulous if dry report of differing approaches to translating the Bible from the Septuagint and Jerome through to Erasmus and Luther. Style is not addressed.

Naomi Seidman, *Faithful Renderings: Jewish-Christian Difference and the Politics of Translation*, University of Chicago Press, 2006. A perceptive account of Bible translations (and of a few other translations as well) from the Septuagint to the present, with special attention to the ways in which they are driven by ideological or theological agendas.

INDEX

alliteration, 72–76, 78, 80, 93, 97, 102

Andrewes, Launcelot, 3

Aquinas, Thomas, 52

Atwood, Margaret, 17

Auerbach, Erich, 103–4

Bakhtin, Mikhail, 104

Balzac, Honoré de, 45

Bellow, Saul, 16

Bible: Geneva Bible, xii, 1–2; Jewish Publication Society (JPS) version, 6, 13, 14, 15, 18–19, 20, 21, 35, 56–57, 92, 100, 109, 111–15, 120; King James Version, xi–xii, 2–11, 17, 29, 43, 48–49, 51, 64, 70–71, 78, 83–85, 89, 91–92, 96–99, 105, 110, 113, 116, 120; New English Bible, 91; New Jerusalem Bible, 5–6, 13, 14, 20, 21, 51, 90–92, 96, 99, 105, 111, 115, 117; Revised English Bible, 5, 13, 14, 19, 20, 21, 42, 58–63, 92, 99–100, 111, 117, 119; Septuagint translation, 14; Tyndale Bible, 1–2, 49, 110. *See also* modern translators' problems

Bible, books of: Genesis, x–xii, 5–6, 8, 16, 17–18, 25, 27–29, 31, 32–33, 39–44, 46, 49–50, 54–56, 58–63, 68, 70–72, 82–83, 103, 104–16; Exodus, 15, 19, 47–48, 50, 51, 52, 88–91; Leviticus, xiii, 11; Deuteronomy, 33–34, 71, 88; Judges, 13, 14, 15, 30, 41, 47, 54, 67, 116–19; Ruth, 46; Samuel, xii, 12–15, 20–22, 48, 52, 56–58, 66—67, 85–88, 109; Kings, xii, 46; Chronicles, 46; Ezra-Nehemiah, 46; Esther, 46; Job, 8, 9, 15, 35, 37–38, 68–70, 73–74, 86, 96–97; Psalms, xiii, xv, 8–9, 15, 23, 36, 51, 72, 73, 75–76, 92–93, 95, 98–102; Proverbs, 67–68; Ecclesiastes, 2, 46; Song of Songs, 18–19, 48, 76; Isaiah, xiii–xiv, 36–37, 48, 72–73, 74–75, 77–80, 95–96; Jeremiah, 34–35, 80; Ezekiel, 79–80; Daniel, 46; Joel, 78–79; Jonah, 46; Zephaniah, 77; New Testament, 1, 25

biblical philology (and specialization), 10–17, 46–47

Bloch, Ariel and Chana, 19, 48

Borchardt, Georges, xi

Buber, Martin, 23–25, 84, 118

construct state, 47

dialogue, 19, 32, 50, 56, 103–21; anticipations of the novel, 103–4; expressive syntax in, 36, 106, 110, 119; gestures toward the colloquial, 53, 104–5; mimetic distortions of language, 104

Dickens, Charles, 45

Dickinson, Emily, 63

diction. *See* word choice

Donne, John, 65–66

etymology, 24–25, 47, 49

explanatory translations, 7, 21, 91, 93

Fagles, Robert, 94

Faulkner, William, 17

Fielding, Henry, 11
Flaubert, Gustave, 45
Forman, Steve, x–xi, xii–xiii
Fox, Everett, 24–25, 83–84
free indirect discourse, 39–40
Frost, Robert, 63

"God" in Hebrew, 50–53, 106;
   "Shaddai," 69, 78–79

Hemingway, Ernest, 6, 17, 63–64
heteroglossia, 104
hineh (presentative), 40, 41, 42
Homer, 14, 53, 54, 104; translations
   of, 93–94, 95, 102

Ibn Ezra, Abraham, xi, 8
idioms, 2, 17, 24
italics (in King James Version), 3–4

James, Henry, 45
James I, 2, 3, 10, 98
Joyce, James, 17

Keats, John, 31, 55

laconic narrative, 44
Lafrance, Adrienne, 32
Lattimore, Richmond, 94, 95
literalism and fidelity, 3–4, 23, 98,
   102, 116

Maimonides, 52
Marks, Herbert, 7
McEwan, Ian, 16
Melville, Herman, 84–85, 88
Merwin, W. S., 16
modern translators' problems:
   avoidance of anthropomorphism,
   51–52; condescension, 62–63,
   92–93; diction lapses, 5, 12, 53–
   58, 60–61, 91, 118, 120; etymology
   overreliance, 24–25; explanatory
   impulse, 5–7, 19, 21, 41, 58, 113,
117; failure to consider context,
13–15, 19, 21; failure to represent
Hebrew literary structures, 27–
28, 32–33; literary and cultural
limitations, 10–12, 16–19, 84;
mistranslations and howlers,
7–8, 13–15, 48–50; obtrusively
modern language, 11, 25–26, 97;
parataxis avoidance, 4, 6, 16, 28–
29; philological overreliance, 11–
15, 46–47; rhythm avoidance, 76,
84–85, 97; sex and body functions avoidance, 19, 48, 59, 60,
110–12

Nabokov, Vladimir, 17

parallelism, 4, 6, 15, 28–29, 54
parataxis, 4, 6, 17, 28–31, 90
Peterson, Eugene, 25–26
Pope, Alexander, 94, 102
prose vs. poetry distinction, 4–5,
   8–10, 12; syntax and, 34–35, 37–
   38; word choice and, 53–54, 75
Psalter, The (1994), 23
puns. *See* word play

Rashi (Rabbi Shlomo Yitzchaki), xi,
   8, 39, 54
Rendsburg, Gary, 109–10
repetition, 5, 12, 16, 20–22, 54, 67,
   70, 118
rhythm, xiv, xv, 2, 6, 24, 82–102;
   compactness and, 53, 87, 89–90,
   92, 93, 95; inconsistent represen-
   tations in, 83, 91–92, 97–98;
   losses through arythmia in, 84,
   92, 98; in poetry, 53, 91, 92–102;
   relation to meaning, 85, 95
Rosenzweig, Franz, 23–25, 84, 118
Roth, Philip, 17

Shakespeare, William, 55, 85–86, 88,
   120

"soul" mistranslations, 7–8, 48

sound play, xv, 65–81, 93; in creation story, 71–72; in Song of Deborah, 54. *See also* word play

Star Wars syntax, 32

Stendhal, 10–11

style, xiv–xvi, 6, 9, 12, 17, 44, 121

syntax, xiii–xvi, 4, 9, 10, 27–44; chiasm, 35–36, 37; fronting, 32–34, 36–37, 110, 119; inversion, 9, 31–34, 36–38; significance of Hebrew word order, 31–32, 37, 39, 110, 119–20

"to be" nonequivalence in Hebrew, 4–5, 95

translation theory: "domesticating" vs. "foreignizing" translations, 22–23; "dynamic equivalence," 23

Updike, John, xi

Venuti, Lawrence, 22

vocabulary. *See* word choice

Whitman, Walt, 9

Woolf, Virginia, 17

word choice, xiv, xv, 2, 4–5, 6, 12, 45–64; levels of diction in Hebrew, 53, 55–56, 104

word play, xiii–xiv, xv, 65–81

A NOTE ON THE TYPE

{⊶⊷}

THIS BOOK has been composed in Miller, a Scotch Roman typeface designed by Matthew Carter and first released by Font Bureau in 1997. It resembles Monticello, the typeface developed for The Papers of Thomas Jefferson in the 1940s by C. H. Griffith and P. J. Conkwright and reinterpreted in digital form by Carter in 2003.

Pleasant Jefferson ("P. J.") Conkwright (1905–1986) was Typographer at Princeton University Press from 1939 to 1970. He was an acclaimed book designer and AIGA Medalist.

The ornament used throughout this book was designed by Pierre Simon Fournier (1712–1768) and was a favorite of Conkwright's, used in his design of the *Princeton University Library Chronicle.*